I0025048

Epher Whitaker

History of Southold, L.I.

Its first century. Vol. 1

Epher Whitaker

History of Southold, L.I.
Its first century. Vol. 1

ISBN/EAN: 9783337403362

Printed in Europe, USA, Canada, Australia, Japan

Cover: Foto ©ninafisch / pixelio.de

More available books at **www.hansebooks.com**

HISTORY

OF

SOUTHOLD, L. I.

ITS FIRST CENTURY.

BY THE

REV. EPHER WHITAKER, D. D.,

Pastor of the First Church of Southold, Councilor of the Long Island
Historical Society, Corresponding Member of the New
York Genealogical and Biographical Society, etc.

SOUTHOLD:
PRINTED FOR THE AUTHOR.
1881.

TO

MR. THOMAS R. TROWBRIDGE

AND

MR. WILLIAM H. H. MOORE,

WHO MAY SEVERALLY REPRESENT THE PLACES OF THEIR
BIRTH, THE CENTRAL CITY AND THE REMOTEST
TOWN OF

THE NEW HAVEN COLONY,

AND WHOSE APPRECIATION AND GENEROSITY HAVE CHEERED
THE PREPARATION OF THIS VOLUME, IT IS MOST
RESPECTFULLY AND GRATEFULLY
DEDICATED BY

THE AUTHOR.

PREFACE.

The acquisition of the greater part of the knowledge contained in this volume has resulted from the duties and necessities of the Christian ministry in the pastoral care of the First Church of Southold for the last thirty years. The preparation of the book for the press has been the rest and recreation of many a weary hour during most of this ministry. Various hindrances have resisted the accomplishment of the undertaking, and caused a less orderly arrangement of the materials of the work, as well as a less vigorous and attractive style, than could be desired; but the belief is cherished, that the imperfections of the book, however clearly seen by the reader, and deeply felt by the writer, should not forbid its publication. For it is highly desirable, that the early life and worth—the purpose,

spirit, circumstances, deeds and sufferings—
in a word, the History of the people of this
Town should be so presented, that its main
features, at least, may be easily known from
generation to generation. The field on which
labor for this end has been expended is the
Past; but the harvest desired is for the Future.
The work aims to supply the wants of posterity not less than to satisfy the requirements
of the present time. He who plants a tree
that will yield good fruit after the sod has covered him, may render an acceptable service
to many, even though not one of his own generation profits by his caré and forethought for
the welfare and comfort of his successors;
and he who provides the means which will
contribute to gratify the wholesome desires
and supply the mental and moral wants of
those who shall live in coming years, may
perhaps not labor in vain. It is altogether
fit, that the Christian minister should look
forward. The objects of his chief thought
and concern have the closest relations to the
endless Future; and it is most reasonable,
that he should take the liveliest interest in the
wants, the prosperity, the comfort, the virtue
and the piety of the generations to come.

These motives have produced this book. Some parts of it may be found in two Papers, prepared by invitation of the Long Island Historical Society, and read in its meetings, respectively on " The First Church of Southold," and on " The First Pastor of Southold ; " and in a Paper, prepared by invitation of the New Haven Colony Historical Society, and read before it, on " The Early History of Southold." The latter is printed in the Second Volume of the Society's Papers.

The subject-matter of this History has been drawn from so many sources, both original and secondary, that it is impossible to name them all. Many of them are indicated in the successive chapters; and it is believed, that the statements based upon them, are in a high degree trustworthy.

Special acknowledgments, justly due, are hereby gratefully tendered, to Mr. GEORGE HANNAH, Librarian of the Long Island Historical Society, and his Assistants ; to the Rev. ADDISON C. V. SCHENCK, of the Presbyterian Historical Society ; and to Mr. FREDERICK SAUNDERS, of the Astor Library, for the utmost courtesy and kindness. Thanks are also due, and gratefully tendered, to the Rev.

WILLIAM F. WHITAKER, Pastor of the St. Cloud
Presbyterian Church, Orange, New Jersey,
for his generous aid in conducting the volume
through the press.

It is hoped that the book will be all the
more acceptable by reason of its several en-
gravings, which are in the highest degree ef-
fective as illustrations.

There are abundant materials at hand for
an interesting History of the Second Century
of Southold ; but whether a second volume
shall be prepared for the press, time must
determine.   E. W.

SOUTHOLD, July 2, 1881.

CONTENTS.

Conklin—Isaac Arnold—Thomas Moore—Capt. John
Underhill—Barnabas Wines—John Budd—Purchase from
the Indians—by the New Haven Government, August,
1640—Lease from James Farrett to Matthew Sunderland,
June, 1639—Deed from Lord Sterling's agent to Richard
Jackson, August 15, 1640—Planting of Southold, Southampton, New Haven—Purchase of Indian titles by Englishmen in New England—In Plymouth, Wethersfield,
Hartford, New Haven, New York—On Long Island in
Southold, Southampton, Jamaica—Southold the first
Town settled on Long Island—Older than Southampton
in all essential points—Hon. Henry A. Reeves's statement—Southold's Indian name—Its early " freeholders
and inhabitants "—Character and work of the early settlers—Their names—Their religious life—Some remove
to other places—Thomas Baker, Jeremiah Meacham and
George Miller to Easthampton—John Tucker, William
Fanley, John Budd, Arthur Smyth, Robert Akerly and
John Frost to Brookhaven—Capt. John Underhill to
Oyster Bay—Letter from him—His wife's sister, Hannah Feke, marries John Bowne—Thomas Stevenson
moves to Newtown—Thomas Benedict to Huntington,
to Jamaica, and lastly to Norwalk, Conn.—John Bayley
to Jamaica, and perhaps to Elizabeth, N. J.—William
Cramer, John Dickerson, John Haines, William Johnson, Jeffrey Jones, Evan Salisbury, Barnabas Wines, Jr.,
and Thomas Youngs to Elizabeth, N. J.—Eminent descendants of the early settlers—Youngses, Wellses, Hor-
tons, Dickinsons, Wineses—Letter from the Rev. Dr. E.
C. Wines—Corwins, Swezeys, Sewards—Some of the
early inhabitants restless—Most and best planted for Religion—Rev. Dr. Leonard Bacon's statement—Southold's
first church and cemetery—Southold's choice of the
New Haven Jurisdiction—Southampton and Easthampton join Connecticut—Southold's purpose—Determination to maintain its rights—Injuries to the Puritans

CHAPTER II.

records—For collecting taxes—For assigning seats in
the Meeting House according to rank, age, office, &c.—
For making vice and crime pay expenses—For keeping
Town streets in good condition—For the wharf at the
Head of the Harbor—For pasturing cattle—For building
a wind mill on Pine Neck—Adjustment of boundaries
with Southampton—Sale of a vessel—Price of grain and
provisions—Bequest of children—Laws for boats, canoes,
skiffs—For prohibiting sale of dogs, rum and arms to
Indians—For paying premiums to destroyers of wolves,
foxes and other " varment "—Election of Selectmen—
Conditions of selling real estate—Mildness of the criminal code—Superiority to old abuses—The Bible the general law—Less than twenty crimes punished by death
here instead of hundreds in England—Popular knowledge of the general law—Bill of Rights—Provisions for
public education—For public worship—Penalties for
disturbing it—Conviction and punishment of Humphrey
Norton—Sales of property must be recorded—Registry
of births, marriages and deaths—Records open to inspection and transcript—All legal proceedings to be put on
record—Distribution of property among heirs—Two
causes for divorce—Justice and kindness towards the savages—Hostilities and suffering from national wars—Military regulations—Burdens of the people born for others—Attempts to invade their liberties—Character of
Charles II.—Character of the first settler and pastor of
Southold—His death and that of William Wells—The
first pastor's grave—Inscription on his tomb-stone—Inventory on his property—Order of administration to his
widow—His children—His theology—Monuments of
early settlers, Youngs, Horton, Wells, Dickinson, Conklin, and others—The original cemetery—Site of the first
Meeting House—Structure of this building—Its various
uses—Its hallowed associations.

CHAPTER III.

1

PART II.—1674-1717.

CHAPTER IV.

The second pastor, Rev, Joshua Hobart—His ancestry—His father, Rev. Peter Hobart, in England, in
America, at Hingham, Mass.—Rev. Peter Hobart's sons
in the ministry—Letter from the Hon. Solomon Lincoln,

CHAPTER V.

holders Inhabitants of the Town—No change of the religious liberties of the people—Gradual enlargement of
the territory of the Town by purchase from the savages—Indian Deed for the whole territory of the Town—
Town Patent-Deed of the Patentees to the Freeholders
Inhabitants—Law for the incorporation of the Commoners—Amendment thereto—The second pastor prominent in civil, industrial and medical affairs—The first
medical practitioner—Privileges granted to the chief
men—A new Meeting House built in 1684—The old
House made a County Prison—The Horton house enlarged for a County Court House—Picture of the Horton house—The site of the former church edifices—
Changes indicated by the tax list of 1683—Names that
disappeared between 1675 and 1683—New names—Com-
parative permanence of family names—The rich more
enduring than the poor—Purchase of John Herbert's
land in 1697 for the use of the Minister—John Herbert
and his father John Herbert—He makes in 1699 a deed
for the land on which stand the present Church and parsonage—This land in the hands of the Trustees of the
First Church by virtue of their incorporation in 1784—
Hon. Ezra L'Hommedieu, a member of the Southold
Church, probably the author of the State law for their
incorporation—Provisions of the law—Election of the
first Board—Certificate of incorporation—The earliest on
Long Island—The attesting Judge, Thomas Youngs, of
Southold—The Board perpetual—The property used for
its proper purposes—Gallery built in the east end of the
Meeting House in 1699; in the west end in 1700—Car-
penters' bills—Bills for care of the Meeting House—The
Town's purchase of the pastor's homestead in 1701—
Probable reasons therefor—This house repaired in 1702—
Puritans in the Province compelled to be cautious—
Lord Cornbury's government—Attempt to establish the
Episcopal church—Trinity church, New York, opened in

PART III.—1720-1736.

CHAPTER VI.

Third Pastor, Rev. Benjamin Woolsey—Relation of
Yarmouth, England, to Southold—Mr. Woolsey's ances-
try—Their relations to Rev. Dr. Ames, Rev. Messrs.
Hugh Peters, of Salem, Thomas Hooker, of Hartford,

and others—Some of them come to Salem—Mr. Woolsey's grandfather becomes a resident of New York—
Moves to Jamaica—Chosen Town Clerk, 1673—Mr.
Woolsey's father, George, Jr., becomes prominent in Jamaica—George Woolsey, 3d, moves to Pennington, New
Jersey—IIis descendants there—Our third Pastor born
in Jamaica—His education at Yale College—His marriage—Early years of his Ministry in various places—
Complaint against Gov. Hunter for allowing him to
preach in the Episcopal church, Hopewell, N. J.—His
installation in Southold, July, 1720—Fruits of his Ministry—Rev. Abner Reeve—His education at Yale—Ilis
Ministry—His sons, Rev. Ezra Reeve and Judge Tapping Reeve—Rev. Simon Horton—His education at
Yale—His Ministry in Newtown, L. I. and elsewhere—
Rev. Azariah Horton—His education at Yale—Missionary to the Indians—His mother Mary (Tuthill) Horton
and her family—His relations to the Edinburgh " Society for Propagating Christian Knowledge " — Extracts
from the Minutes of this Society—His Journals—His
preparation of the Indians for the Rev. David Brainerd
at Easton, Pa.— His complaints against "the Separates "—He becomes the first Pastor of Madison, N. J.—
His death—His grave and epitaph—His descendants—
Judge Thomas Youngs—Ilis education at Yale—Ilis
civil and judicial services—His death—IIis ancestry—
His marriage—His home—His large possessions of
land—His son Thomas—His later posterity—Rev. David
Youngs—His education at Yale—His pastorate at Brook-
Haven—His death—Migration from Southold—To Chester, N. J., for example—Historic sketch of that place—
Public worship in Orient—Mattituck Church organized,
1715—Its first pastor, Rev. Joseph Lamb—His removal
to Basking Ridge, N. J.—His relations to the Hon. Henry Southard—a Long Islander—to Hon. Samuel
L. Southard—Historical sketch of Basking Ridge—

PART IV.—1736-1740.

CHAPTER VII.

riages of John Lloyd and Sarah Woolsey—M. T. Woolsey's daughter Rebekah marries James Hillhouse—
James Hillhouse and his descendants—M. L. Woolsey's
services in the Revolutionary War and thereafter—His
marriage, and connections thereby—His son M. T.
Woolsey in the U. S. Navy—Our third Pastor's second
son, Benjamin—His education at Yale—His marriages—
His children—Their connections and posterity—Rev.
Timothy Dwight, D. D., President of Yale College—
William W. Woolsey—His daughter Elizabeth, mother
of Major Theodore Winthrop—His son John M. Wool-
sey, father of Sarah Chauncey Woolsey, " Susan Cool-
idge "—Our third pastor's great grandson, Theodore
Dwight Woolsey, D. D., LL. D., President of Yale Col-
lege, son of W. W. Woolsey—President Woolsey's son
Theodore S. Woolsey, Professor of International Law in
Yale College—Rev. Benjamin Woolsey's granddaughter
Elizabeth, daughter of Benjamin, marries William Dun-
lap, the artist—Other descendants in the female lines,
Lt. Gov. John Broome, Chancellor William T. McCoun,
Rear Admiral S. L. Breese ; Hon. Sidney Breese, Chief
Justice of Illinois, U. S. Senator ; Sarah Elizabeth Gris-
wold, wife of Prof. Morse, Inventor of the Telegraph ;
Arthur Breese, U. S. Navy ; Mary Welles Davenport,
wife of James Boorman ; George Welles McClure, U. S.
Army ; Henry Welles, Judge of N. Y. Supreme Court ;
Abigail Woolsey Welles, wife of the Rev. Dr. Henry G.
Ludlow and mother of the well known authors Fitszhugh
Ludlow and Helen W. Ludlow—Rev. James Davenport
becomes Pastor of Southold after Mr. Woolsey's resig-
nation—His ancestry—His birth in Stamford, Conn.—
His education at Yale—His studies for the Ministry—
His ill health—His Ministry in Southold, 1738-1739—His
call in 1738 to Maidenhead and Hopewell, N. J.—His
preference for Southold—His remarkable career in the
erratic period of his Ministry—His excellent character

PART I.

PERIOD OF THE MINISTRY OF THE REV. JOHN YOUNGS.

---

1 6 4 0 – 1 6 7 2 .

CHAPTER I.

There is a peculiar attraction which draws
the thoughts and affections of men to the
sources of any stream, that having continued
to flow from age to age, still spreads its benign influences far and wide, with ever-in-
creasing volume and usefulness. And the ex-
plorations of the Nile or the Amazon are not
more charming to some minds than the inves-
tigation of the places, conditions, circumstances and causes of the fountains and cur-
rents of those historic movements which have
contributed to shape the destiny and promote
the welfare of our country and our race.
2

The origin, direction and character of the smallest streams are full of interest to every man who would thoroughly understand the life and wealth which the broader and deeper river of our national and Christian history now bears and carries forward upon its ample and generous bosom.

It may be superfluous to remark, that the history of permanent Christian institutions, in this country, before the close of a third of the seventeenth century, presents only

> " The baby figures of the giant mass
> Of things to come at large."

It is at this point that we come upon a record which directly pertains to the early history of Southold, Long Island.   It is in these words :

" The examination of John Yonge, of St. Margaretts, Suff, minister aged 35 years and Joan his wife aged 34 yeares with 6 children John, Thomas, Anne, Rachel, Marey and Joseph are desirous to passe fo Salam in N England to inhabit

" This man was forbyden passage by the commissioners and went not from Yarmouth."

For this record of the royal Commissioners of Emigration, see Massachusetts Hist. Society's Col.—Fourth Series, vol. I., page 101.

This is a record of 1633, if the record correctly gives his age 35 years, and if he was 74 years of age at his death in 1672, as the inscription on his tombstone relates. But in the "Indexes of Southold," by Charles B. Moore, Esq., it is held, that Mr. Youngs's attempt to emigrate from Yarmouth occurred May 11, 1637, as stated in the copy of the English Record made for Mr. Savage. The Commissioners of Emigration were appointed, it is believed, in 1634. See the New York Genealogical and Biographical Record, vol. 4, p. 16. The minister, whose passage from Yarmouth to Salem the Commissioners forbade only a few years after the organization of the earliest church in New England, seems to have had no desire to return to St. Margaret's in Suffolk.

But where was this St. Margaret's? For there were more than one St. Margaret's in Suffolk. We should perhaps most naturally refer this record to St. Margaret's of Southolt in the Hundred of Hoxne, Suffolk. The name

of the place is printed Southold in Camden.
In Lewis's Topographical Dictionary of England, fifth edition, 1842, it is described as follows: " SOUTHOLT, (St. Margaret) a parish in the union and hundred of Hoxne, E.
Division of the County of Suffolk, 5 miles
(S. E. by S.) from Eye; containing 211 inhabitants. The living is a perpetual curacy,
endowed with the great tithes, and annexed
to the rectory of Worlingworth: the tithes
have been commuted to a rent–charge of
£237.10. A school is supported out of the
rents of town lands, the proceeds of which,
amounting to about £100 per annum, are applied to the repairs of the church, and to the
general purposes of the parish." Investiga-
tion seems to show, that Mr. Youngs never
had charge of this church and parish. In re-
ply to a letter making inquiry as to Mr.
Youngs's incumbency of this St. Margaret's,
previous to his emigration to this country, the
Reverend Rector of Worlingworth most courteously gave the following evidence, that Mr.
Youngs was not at any time during the seventeenth century an incumbent of that parish :

" Worlingworth Rectory,
Wickham Market,
Suffolk, February, 18, 1879.

Dear Sir :—I have been waiting for an answer, which I enclose, from the Bishop of Norwich's Registrar (Mr. Bonsly) as to the names of the Incumbents at the time you mention. I am sorry to say Mr. Youngs's name does not appear. Yet St. Margaret's and Southolt—spelt in Camden Southold—are certainly curious coincidences to say the least. Trusting you will excuse my long delay, I am, Dear Sir, respectfully,
FRED. FRENCH,
Rector of Worlingworth and Southolt, Suffolk.
To the Rev. Epher Whitaker,
Southold, Suffolk Co.,
New York, U. S. A."

The Rev. Rector's letter from the Rev. W. T. Bonsly, the Registrar of the Diocese of Norwich, is this :

" Diocesan Registry, Norwich,
17 February, 1879.

Dear Sir :—The question in your letter of the 4th inst. whether the Rev. John Youngs was Rector of Southold or South(w)old *
* * * is easily answered in the negative. * * *
I have referred to Dr. Tanner's list of Incumbents of Worlingworth with Southolt. It does not contain the name of John Young.

The Incumbents, mentioned by him, in the
17th century, are
Miles Spencer
1623 Philip Tynck
Tickle turned out 1643.
1661 Hugh Roberts
1666 John Ward
1673 Thos. Colman.
I return Mr. Whitaker's letter.
Yours faithfully,
W. T. BONSLY.
The Revd. F. French."

There is another St. Margaret's in Suffolk
in the Hundred of Wangford. It is about
midway between Halesworth and Bungay, and
some six miles from each. It is St. Margaret's Ilketshall. But nothing has been found
to show that the Rev. John Youngs was ever
the minister of that place. Thomas Young,
the teacher of John Milton, was from 1630 to
1655 the rector of Stow-Market, a large borough and polling place in the central part of
Suffolk County, on the line of the railroad
from London by way of Ipswich and Norwich
to Yarmouth. It is most likely that our first
pastor was connected in some way with St.
Margaret's in the village of Reydon, near the
sea-coast, and in the Hundred of Blything.

Wangford is on the great post-road between Ipswich and Yarmouth, and Southwold is on the shore of the sea about five or six miles southeast of Wangford. Reydon is about midway between these two places. An important letter recently sent from New Jersey and plainly directed to Southold, Suffolk County, Long Island, reached its destination in twenty-one days with the postmarks of both Wangford and Southwold, England, upon it. In some books and maps published in the seventeenth century, and found in the Presbyterian Historical Society's Library in Philadelphia, Southwold, England, is printed " Southould " and " Sowolde." On an eminence in Southwold, so as to look out upon the North Sea, a fine church edifice was built in 1460 and dedicated to St. Edmunds. This was a chapel annexed to the vicarage of Reydon, and the curate of this chapel was appointed by the vicar of Reydon, who from 1611 to his death in 1626 was the Rev. Christopher Young. His successor, appointed the next year, was the Rev. John Goldsmith. From this neighborhood it is highly probable that Christopher Youngs of Massachusetts came to America, and to this St. Margaret's of Reydon it may be supposed

that the Rev. John Youngs belonged when he
purposed to cross the ocean for Salem in New
England to inhabit.   He may have ministered
in Southwold as a curate of the vicar of St.
Margaret's in Reydon.   Edward Yonges, a
vicar, was in Southwold in 1616.   It is stated
by Charles B. Moore, Esq., that our first pastor " had the official record of being forbidden passage in the Mary Ann of Yarmouth—
the vessel in which he proposed to sail in 1637
from Yarmouth to Salem, with Mrs. Ames,
and with his own wife and children.   Some of
his parishoners came in that vessel, and probably his family, for they soon arrived."   He
may have made the voyage by way of Holland.   " He appeared at Salem, Massachusetts, at the same time with ' the widow Ames'
and her sons.   Lands were voted to be given
to him if he would stay at Salem, and also to
her, and to the widow Paine, who, with others,
came over in the Mary Ann when he was
stopped.   Mr. Youngs did not stay long at
Salem, but appeared soon at New Haven with
Mr. Davenport."   See the New York Genealogical and Biographical Record, vol. 3, p.
164, vol. 4, p. 16.   These facts make it highly probable that our first pastor was a kins-

man of the vicar of Reydon, and that our Puritan town, the oldest on Long Island, was
named Southold on account of his connection
with Southould or Southwold in England.
The name of the county also was taken of
course from Suffolk County, England. Undoubtedly the various modes of writing the
names as Southold, Southhold, Southould,
Southwold, Sowolde, had far more relation to
the written than to the oral use.

After the Rev. John Youngs was forbidden
to sail for New England from Yarmouth just
at the point where England thrusts the coast-
line deepest into the German ocean, perhaps
he retired a day's journey directly inland toward the west, and became the pastor of a
church at Hingham, in Norfolk County, a parish some ten or twelve miles nearly west of
the city of Norwich.

Trumbull, in his History of Connecticut,
says that "New Haven, or their confederates,
purchased and settled Yennycock, [Southold]
on Long Island. Mr. John Youngs, who had
been a minister at Hingham, in England,
came over with a considerable part of his
church, and here fixed his residence. He
gathered his church anew on the 21st of Octo-

3

ber, [1640,] and the planters united them-
selves with New Haven." "Some of the
principal men were the Reverend Mr. Youngs,
Mr. William Wells, Mr. Barnabas Horton,
Thomas Mapes, John Tuthill, and Matthias
Corwin."

There is no trace of evidence known to me
that all of these men ever resided in New
Haven.

Thompson, in his History of Long Island,
says that the Rev. John Youngs "organized a
church at New Haven, and they, with others
willing to accompany them, commenced the
settlement of this town." But Thompson
gives no authority for this statement, and it is
manifestly unhistorical. It was "here" at
Southold that "he gathered his church
anew;" for it was "here" at Southold that
he "fixed his residence;" and the church
which he gathered anew was not a church organized in New Haven; but it was organized
in Southold where he fixed his residence.

Mr. Augustus Griffin, in his "Journal,"
tells a lively story of the settlement of Southold—how a company of thirteen men with
their families left England about the year
1638; after some weeks, arrived at New Ha-

ven, "then a small village in the then colony of Connecticut;" how they remained there about two years, until early in the autumn of 1640, when they all embarked in a vessel with their families, effects, and provisions enough to supply them for the coming win- ter, and sailed to Southold and made their dwellings here. The names of these thirteen men, Mr. Griffin says, were Rev. John Youngs, Barnabas Horton, William Wells, Esq., Peter Hallock, John Tuthill, Richard Terry, Thomas Mapes, Matthias Corwin, Robert Akerly, Ja- cob Corey, John Conkline, Isaac Arnold, John Budd. "These men," he adds, "with their families, were the first of any civilized nation that had made the attempt to settle on the east end of Long Island. This took place in the early part of September 1640."

The venerable man who wrote the above when he was ninety years of age, was genial, kindly, and imaginative, and he drew largely for his facts upon his fancy in making the sketch of the settlement and early history of South- old. No company of thirteen men, including these whose names he gives, ever crossed the ocean in the same vessel, or lived two years together in New Haven, or sailed to Southold either at the time or in the manner that he describes in the first pages of his romantic narrative; nor was New Haven at that time in the then colony of Connecticut. His "thirteen adventurers" include men of different generations, and some of them were scarcely born in 1640. There is only a tradition that one of them was ever in Southold at any time.

These facts are now well known in respect to them, namely:

William Wells, Esq., son of an eminent prebendary of the cathedral of Norwich, who was also the Rector of the most magnificent and splendid church in that city, left England, it is believed, June 19th, 1635, in the same vessel with John Bayley, another of the early settlers of Southold, who in 1664 became the first of three purchasers of the Indian title of Elizabeth, New Jersey. Mr. Wells probably came here by way of Lynn, Massachusetts, and not from New Haven. See Moore's "Indexes of Southold" and Hayes's "William Wells of Southold."

Barnabas Horton was not a native of Hingham in Norfolkshire; but of Mouseley in Leicestershire. There is no evidence that he ever was in Hingham, England, or in New Haven, in this country, before he settled at Southold. He may have dwelt in Hampton, Massachusetts, previous to 1640. See the Horton Genealogy, by G. F. Horton, M. D.

The following is the inscription on the massive slab of blue slate, imported from Mouseley, that rests upon the walls which surround his grave:

"Here lieth buried the body of Mr. Barnabas Horton, who was born at Mousely, Leicestershire, old England, and died at Southold, on the 13th day of July, 1680, aged 80 years.

Here lies my body tombed in dust
' Till Christ shall come to raise it with the just ;
My soul ascended to the throne of God,
Where with sweet Jesus now I make abode :
Then hasten after me, my dearest wife,
To be partaker of this blessed life ;
And you, dear children all, follow the Lord,
Hear and obey His public sacred word ;
And in your houses call upon His name,
For oft have I advised you to the same :
Then God will bless you with your children all,
And to this blessed place he will you call.

Heb. XI: 4. 'He being dead, yet speaketh.' "

Peter Hallock was probably the father of William Hallock, and may have come to Southold; but there is only traditional evidence of it. William Hallock, who died on the 28th day of September, 1684, left a record, property and posterity here. He wrote his name Holyoake. But he was probably the ancestor of all the Hallocks and Hallecks in this country. See the Records of the Town of Southold, and William Holyoake's will in the " Hallock Genealogy," by the Rev. William A. Hallock, D. D.

John Tuthill may have come to this place from Hingham, Massachusetts, whence came hither Henry Tuthill, the ancestor of all the Tuthills of Southold. Henry Tuthill settled in Hingham, Massachusetts, in 1637, where he had land which he afterwards sold, probably because of his removal to Southold. His wife survived him, and afterwards became the wife of William Wells, Esq. See Town Records, Book A, folio 105, and Tuthill " Family Meeting," pages 31—33, printed at Sag Harbor, 1867. See also New Haven Colony Records, 2, folio 97.

Richard Terry sailed from England with his elder brothers Thomas and Robert in 1635.

Both Thomas and Richard subsequently made
their homes in Southold. But in 1640 Richard was negotiating with Capt. Howe, of Lynn,
Massachusetts, for a settlement on Long Island, and Capt. Howe, at that time, was plan-
ning to settle Southampton. See Moore's
" Indexes of Southold" and George R. Howell's " History of Southampton, Long Island."

Thomas Mapes was here as early as 1657.
He was a son-in-law of William Purrier, who
was settled in Southold before any record
was made to show the presence and interests
of Mr. Mapes in this place. William Purrier
was of Olney, Buckinghamshire, the parish
which Newton and Cowper have made famous. He sailed from England with his wife
and three children on the first day of April
1635, in the " Hopewell," for New England.
John Cooper and Edmund Farrington of the
same village were his companions on the
voyage. John Cooper settled in Boston,
where he became a " freeman," that is, a
voter, in 1636. He afterwards removed to
New Haven and subsequently became one of
the foremost, wealthy and influential persons
in Southampton, Long Island. He was in
Southold, with his home in Southampton, in

1673. Edmund Farrington settled in Lynn, and afterward became interested in the planting of Southampton, L. I. Thomas Mapes, who seems to have come to Southold later than these Olney men came to Long Island, made his will in 1686. It was proved the next year. See Town Records of Southold. Documents relating to the Colonial History of New York. Moore's Indexes. Howell's Southampton. Hatfield's Elizabeth.

Matthias Corwin settled in Ipswich, Massachusetts, before he made his home in Southold. He received a grant of land—probably a second grant—in that place in 1634. It is evident that he came to Southold by way of New Haven, and may have been in Southold soon after the purchase of the place by the authorities of New Haven. The excellent "Corwin Genealogy," by the Rev. Edward Tanjore Corwin, D. D., refers to the proper authorities, and says on page 161, that "the record at Ipswich notes that he emigrated thence to Long Island." The chapel of the Presbyterian Church, just across the main street from the First Church of Southold, now stands on his house-home lot.

Robert Akerly probably came from Stamford or New Haven to Southold early in the history of this place ; but the precise year is unknown.

Jacob Corey may have been a native of Southold ; for he died here in 1706, more than sixty-five years after the Rev. John Youngs gathered his church anew in this place ; and so far as known, his name appeared for the first time upon the record here in 1667, when he received a deed for a house and lot from John Tuthill. He belonged to the second generation here. See Town Records.

John Conklin doubtless came to Southold from Salem, Massachusetts, where he received, as one of its inhabitants, a grant of four acres of land on the 30th day of May 1649. Before 1655 he removed to Southold and made his home here, apparently in the part of the town called Hashamommuck, though he seems to have retained his lands in Salem ; for in 1683 he gave his son John a deed for them. Previous to this date, he had removed to Huntington, L. I. See Town Records.

Isaac Arnold was born about the time of the settlement of Southold, and died more

than sixty-six years after the organization of
our First Church here.   He became a prominent citizen of the second generation, after
the Rev. John Youngs, William Wells, Esq.,
Matthias Corwin, Barnabas Horton, Thomas
Moore, Capt. John Underhill, Barnabas
Wines, William Purrier, and other chief men
of the first generation had died.

John Budd was in New Haven in 1639,
and for several years thereafter, as the New
Haven Records show ; and most probably he
continued to live there or in England for the
next fifteen years.   He was in the Old
country in 1654.   On his return, he concerned himself in the settlement of Setauket,
Long Island ; but he became a resident of
Southold prior to 1657.   In 1658 he had
much trouble and litigation with some of his
neighbors.   The ample records of this year
show that most precious interests and deep
feelings were touched by a protracted investi-
gation under the provisions of this Town-law
respecting slander :

"Every such person as inhabiteth among
us and shall be found to bee a common tale
bearer, tatler, or busie bodie in idle matters,
forger or coyner of reports, untruths or lyes,

or frequently using provokeinge, rude, unsavorie words, tending to disturb the peace, shall forfeit and pay for every default 10 s."

It was very likely inconveniences arising from the enforcement of this law against one of his neighbors, that led Mr. Budd, in 1659, to sell his house-home lot in this Town, and remove from the place to the main land. In 1661, he purchased land of the Indians in Westchester county, New York, where he settled, and continued to reside until the time of his death, which occurred as early as 1670. See Town Records, New Haven Records, Bolton's History of Westchester County, Moore's Indexes, etc.

The facts on record in respect to these " thirteen men " most thoroughly prove, that there is no historic foundation whatever for the story that they came here together in September 1640 and settled this Town. The facts prove that they never came from England in company ; that they never were together in New Haven, either in 1640, or before or after this date ; that they never came to Southold in the same vessel and at the same time ; that some of them were elsewhere for several years after the settlement ; that

others of them belonged to the second generation of its inhabitants ; that the greater part
of them were never members of the Rev. John
Youngs's church in Hingham, England ; that
they were never organized as a church in New
Haven ; that the story of the settlement to
which Griffin's " Journal " has given currency
is a fiction.

Thompson says that the Rev. John Youngs
" came to New Haven in 1638 ;" and this
statement is likely to hold good.   He also
states, that " the Governor of New Haven
Theophilus Eaton, and the authorities there
had not only aided the first settlers in their
negotiations about the purchase of the soil,
but actually took the conveyance in their own
names, and exercised a limited control over
the territory for several years."   These statements rest immovably on the New Haven Records.

On the 18th of June, 1639, Matthew Sunderland leased of James Farrett lands which
are in the town of Southold.   On the 4th of
September, 1639, he took a receipt for rent
paid thereon.   The next year he improved the
land and paid rent thereon a second time,
namely, September 9th, 1640.   After his death,

his widow retained posession of his improvements; and in 1649, having previously married William Salmon, her second husband and
her children took the personal property and
claimed the land under the lease from Farrett.
See the Town Records. Farrett's first transaction with the Southampton people was a
year later than with Sunderland—one being
June 18, 1639, and the other being June 12,
1640.

Richard Jackson was appointed in Massachusetts, 20th November, 1637, on a committee to lay off Sudbury. In March, 1638, another man, named Oliver, was appointed in
his place. On the 15th of August, 1640, he
obtained a deed from Lord Sterling's agent,
James Farrett, for lands which he had purchased in this Town. This was earlier than
Stirling's deed to Southampton. On the 25th
of the October, 1640, he sold this land with
his house upon it and other improvements to
Thomas Weatherby, mariner, for £15 sterling.
Weatherby subsequently sold it to Stephen
Goodyear, the eminent merchant of New Haven; and Goodyear with title from Weatherby, Jackson, and the Indians, sold it to John
Ketcham, by whom it was conveyed to Thomas

4

Moore, in the possession of whose descendants
and heirs it remains, it is believed, until this
day.   See Goodyear's deed in the Town Records.

This sale of his land with his dwelling house
and other improvements by Jackson was made
four days after the Rev. John Youngs gathered his church anew in this place.

It is not known how many other settlers
were here in 1639 and the following year, before the church was organized on the 21st of
October 1640.   In the planting of the adjoining Town of Southampton, it would appear
that some of the men at least were on the soil
several months before the formation of their
church in November, a month later than the
organization of the First Church of Southold.
The church and town here were in the closest
relations with New Haven ; and the first settlers of the latter place landed on the site
chosen for their plantation the 15th of April,
1638, (O. S.) ; but it was not until August
21st, 1639, that the church was fully organized.
See its Manual for the year 1867.   The anal-
ogy of the neighboring settlements, the known
facts, and the nature of the case, leave no
doubt, that some of the early settlers of South-

old were here many months, and perhaps two years before the organization of the church on the 21st of October, 1640. We trace them on their way hither through other parts of New England, from 1635 onward. Some of them removed from other places during the years 1638 and 1639, and probably came here about the same time.

It was not the custom of the early settlers of New England and other parts of the country to purchase the Indian title and afterwards begin the settlement. On the contrary, the settlements were first begun, and subsequently the settlers engaged in trade with the Indians; and when it became convenient, they purchased the Indian title to the land which they had already occupied. So it was done at Plymouth, and Wethersfield, and Hartford, and New Haven, and New York, and many other places. So it was done on Long Island at Southold, Southampton, Jamaica, and elsewhere. The purchase of Southold was made of the Indians here as early at least as August, 1640, and it is simply preposterous to suppose that the earliest settlers, the Rev. John Youngs and his companions, came here and begun the settlement of the Town at a

later date.   They were doubtless here several
months, and very likely a whole year, before
the purchase of the Indian title in August,
1640.   There seems to be all-sufficient evidence to support the oft-repeated historic
statement, which is made in the words of the
Rev. Dr. Prime's History, that " Southold was
the first town settled on Long Island."

Mr. George R. Howell, the historian of
Southampton, has recently presented a claim
to this distinction in behalf of that Town.   But
the claim is based upon the unfounded sup-
position, that there were no settlers in the
Town of Southold previous to the autumn of
1640, about the time of the organization of
the church in October, (which the Hon. Silas
Wood, in his "Towns of Long Island," seems
erroneously to regard as the settlement of
the Town), or the claim is put forth on the
ground of an imaginary transfer of an imaginary church or company of men from New
Haven to Southold, as stated by Griffin, " in
the early part of September, 1640."   The
truth is, that the settlement here was so old
in the autumn of 1640, that Richard Jackson,
who had cultivated his land and built his
house and other improvements here, desired

at that time to sell, and did sell, his dwelling house, and all his other improvements, as well as his land within this Town, only four days after the date of the organization of the First Church of Southold.

The facts show that this Town is older than Southampton in all the essential and important tests of settlement, namely:

1. Southold is older than Southampton by the earlier purchase of the territory from the Indians.

2. Southold is older than Southampton by the earlier renting and purchase of land from English owners, and cultivation and improvement thereof, by the first dwellers within the bounds of the Town.

3. Southold is older than Southampton by its union in Civil Government with the Towns of the New Haven Jurisdiction at an earlier date than the union of Southampton with the Colony of Connecticut.

4. Southold is older than Southampton by the earlier organization of its First Church in an age when the political and the religious life and institutions of the people were so closely interwoven.

Thus the long-continued historical statement remains good, that "Southold was the first Town settled on Long Island." It may be added, that in the year 1640 the New Haven Colony made a large purchase of territory on both sides of the Delaware, or South river, and sent thither about fifty families. This purchase seems to have been made after the New Haven Jurisdiction had secured possession of Southold on Long Island across the Sound from the original settlement. See Trumbull's History of Connecticut, Vol. 1, p. 119.

When the Town Records of Southampton were edited, printed and published a few years since, the Hon. Henry A. Reeves, a native of the Town of Southampton and a resident of the Town of Southold, wrote and published in his paper, the Republican Watchman of Greenport, the conclusion which he had formed on this subject after an examination of the Records, and subsequently also to the publication of many columns at different times in his paper for and against the new claim of priority of settlement put forth in behalf of his native Town. He said: "Besides our interest in this volume as ' a son of the soil,' we have examined it with some care in order to find whatever light may be cast by it upon the mooted question of priority of settlement as between the towns of Southold and Southampton, but fail to discover any positive or very satisfactory circumstantial evidence bearing upon the point. Certainly the claim recently advanced on behalf of South-ampton, in opposition to the long and hereto-fore universally accepted tradition (admitting that it is not established upon the basis of exact historic truth), which has presented Southold as the oldest town in the State of New York settled by people of English de-scent, cannot be supported upon mere infer-ences and conjectures. The earliest writings in the Town archives, as published in the First Book of Records, do not furnish any stronger or other proofs of priority than such as are strictly inferential. It may be there are other grounds on which Southold's precedence can be disputed, but they have not yet been brought to our notice."

When Southold became a part of the Juris-diction of the New Haven Colony, the people and government of that plantation sometimes called this Long Island Town by its Indian name Yennecock, or Yennecott, and some-

times by its English name Southold. When
the people of Southold were about to build a
village at the western end of the territory of
the Town, on Wading River, they voted in
Town Meeting that it should be called West
Hold. See Town Records, Book A.

For nearly thirty years past I have been
carefully making a list of the early settlers,
who left written evidence, (in the Town Records; in Deeds conveying lands, or other
property; in Wills; on Tombstones, or other
documents,) that they were full grown men
here within the life-time of the first pastor.
Nearly all named in the list which I have
made were not only residents here, but also
landowners. In the words of the Town Patent, they were " Freeholders and Inhabitants."
Of course there were many who left no written record which has survived them and come
down to us. But the life which they lived
here has gone into the body and soul of those
activities and endurances that have formed
the history and the character of this place.
Though we know not their names, we never-
theless enjoy the fruit of their virtues, and
reap the harvest of their toils. The very fact
that they are unnamed may be owing to their

superior modesty and worth, just as a goodly number of women,—faithful daughters, wives and mothers,—who have left no written record here, doubtless surpassed in patience, industry, virtue and piety many sons, husbands and fathers whose names are thus known. They shall in a future day and thenceforth and forever have their proper and honorable meed when the names, written in the Book of Life, become known to all mankind.

Here is the list, which is believed to be accurate as to all whom it includes :

Robert Akerly,
Isaac Arnold,
Thomas Baker,
John Bayley,
Thomas Benedict,
Richard Benjamin,
Simeon Benjamin,
John Booth,
Richard Brown,
Richard Brown, Jr.,
John Budd,
David Carwithe,
Henry Case,
Roger Cheston,

Richard Clark,
John Conklin,
John Conklin, Jr.,
Jacob Conklin,
Thomas Cooper,
John Corey,
Jacob Corey,
Abraham Corey,
Matthias Corwin,
John Corwin,
Theophilus Corwin,
William Cramer,
Caleb Curtis,
Thomas Curtis,

Philemon Dickerson,
Peter Dickerson,
John Dickerson,
Thomas Dimon,
Nicholas Edes,
John Elton,
Matthias Edwards,
John England,
Jeffrey Esty,
William Fanley,
Benoni Flint,
John Franklin,
John Frost,
Charles Glover,
Samuel Glover,
Ralph Goldsmith,
John Greete,
Samuel Grover,
Simon Grover,
James Haines,
John Haines,
William Hallock,
Richard Harrude,
John Herbert,
John Herbert, Jr.,
James Hildreth,
Barnabas Horton,

Joseph Horton,
Benjamin Horton,
Caleb Horton,
Joshua Horton,
Jonas Houldsworth,
Richard Howell,
Thomas Hutchinson,
Richard Jackson,
Joseph Jennings,
William Johnson,
Jeffrey Jones,
John Ketchum,
John King,
Samuel King,
Thomas Mapes,
Thomas Mapes, Jr.,
Jeremiah Meacham,
Stephen Metcalf,
George Miller,
Thomas Moore,
Benjamin Moore,
Jonathan Moore,
Nathaniel Moore,
Francis Nichols,
Humphrey Norton,
Thomas Osman,
Isaac Overton,

Peter Paine,
John Paine,
John Peakin,
Edward Petty,
William Purrier,
John Racket,
James Reeve,
Thomas Rider,
John Rider,
William Robinson,
Evan Salisbury,
William Salmon,
John Salmon,
Thomas Scudder,
Henry Scudder,
Joshua Silvester,
Richard Skidmore,
Arthur Smyth,
Nathaniel Smyth,
Robert Smyth,
Thomas Stevenson,
Edward Stevenson,
Matthew Sunderland,
John Swezey,
Thomas Terrell,
Richard Terry,
Thomas Terry,

John Terry,
Daniel Terry,
Edward Treadwell,
John Tucker,
Charles Tucker,
Henry Tuthill,
John Tuthill,
John Tuthill, Jr.,
Daniel Turner,
Thomas Tustin,
John Underhill,
Jeremiah Vail,
Jeremiah Vail, Jr.,
Thomas Weatherby,
William Wells,
Henry Whitney,
Thomas Whittier,
John Wiggins,
Abraham Wiggins,
Barnabas Wines,
Barnabas Wines, Jr.,
Samuel Wines,
John Youngs, pastor,
John Youngs, Jr.,
Thomas Youngs,
Samuel Youngs,
Joseph Youngs,

Christopher Youngs,   Joseph Youngs, Jr.,
Joseph Youngs, mariner, Gideon Youngs.--138
    There are 138 names in the list.

It has fallen in my way to learn much of the
history of some of these men and of their descendants of the earlier generations; and I
may say, that there is abundant evidence,
from many sources, that the first settlers were
lovers of liberty and virtue, and had intelligence, and wisdom, and enterprise, and industry, and endurance, and piety enough to make
them, by God's blessing, the worthy founders of a permanent and prosperous Church
and Town.   Throughout the period of twenty-
two years from the first planting of the Town,
it was only the men who were Church members in full communion that could be voters in
the Town Meeting or hold any office of trust
or responsibility in the Town.   Their faith and
patience, their foresight and energy, their pure
worship of God, their high moral life through
obedience to His word, and their supreme
trust in His Son, enabled those who knew them
to say: "The wilderness and the solitary place
shall be glad for them; and the desert shall
rejoice and blossom as the rose." They faith-

fully accomplished the work which Divine Providence committed to their hearts and hands, and left to their successors the precious inheritance that sprang into existence as the fruit of their virtues and their toils.

Of the full-grown men—at least one hundred and thirty-eight—who lived here and left their record in the annals of this Town during the period of the ministry of the first pastor from 1640 to 1672, not a few removed to other places, and became important factors and elements in the settlement and life of other Towns.

Of these, Thomas Baker removed to Easthampton, Long Island. He was one of the settlers and representatives of that Town who obtained in 1649 the title from Gov. Eaton and Gov. Hopkins, these Governors having purchased it the previous year from the native chiefs of Manhanset, (Shelter Island), Montauk, Cutchogue, and Shinnecock. His name is first in the list of residents of Easthampton who in 1660 bought the title of Montauk from the widow and son of the Chief. In this list are also the names of Jeremiah Meacham and George Miller, who had been previously inhabitants of Southold.

5

John Tucker lived on the site of Mr. Barna-
bus Horton Booth's present residence. His
home and land there gave name to the street
which bounds Mr. Booth's property on the
northeast and east from the main street of the
village to the north road. He became one of
the early settlers of the Town of Brookhaven,
Long Island; and so did William Fanley, John
Budd, Arthur Smyth, Robert Akerly and John
Frost.

John Underhill, the famous Captain, ended
his remarkable career in Oyster Bay Township,
Queens County, Long Island. The early history of New England and New York very
clearly shows how he used his sword. While
he was living in Southold he wrote a letter to
John Winthrop, Jr., a part of which letter may
show how he used his pen. It is this:

"SOUTHOULD, L. I.,
            12 of April 1656.
SIR   I was latli at Flusching. Hanna Feke
is to be marrid to a verri gentiele young man,
of gud abiliti, of louli fetture and gud behafior."

This Hanna Feke was a sister of Capt. John
Underhill's wife, Elizabeth Feke—not " Field,"
as Thomson says in his History of Long Island—and, sure enough, she was married to

John Bowne on the 7th day of the next month after Capt. Underhill wrote the above letter to Gov. Winthrop.

Thomas Stevenson, who came to Southold and lived here as early as 1644, was in Hempstead in 1647, when land was assigned to him there. He settled in Newtown as early as 1655.

Thomas Benedict was a native of Nottinghamshire, England. He came early to Southold, and settled in Hashamommuck on the east side of the creek which derived its earliest English name from his own. It was first called Thomas Benedict's creek, later Thomas's creek, then Tom's creek, and now Mill creek. The house in which he lived was not far from the Sound. His five sons and four daughters were born in Southold. He subsequently removed to Huntington, thence to Jamaica, Long Island, and afterwards settled at Norwalk, Connecticut. He was a prominent man in each of these places. See the " Benedict Genealogy," by his descendant, Henry M. Benedict, Esq., of Albany, New York.

John Bayley was born in England in 1617 and resided at Guilford in the jurisdiction of New Haven General Court in 1642. He came to Southold in 1654; sold his dwelling and home lot here in 1661, and removed to Jamaica, Long Island. He was the first who signed the petition to Gov. Nichols for permission to plant Elizabeth, New Jersey, and the first man named in the Indian deed for that place. He was also the first of the four men to whom the patent was granted by the Governor under the Duke of York. He probably never removed from Jamaica to Elizabeth. See the Rev. Dr. Hatfield's History of Elizabeth.

William Cramer moved from Southold to Elizabeth, New Jersey, and so did John Dickerson, John Haines, William Johnson, Jeffrey Jones, Evan Salisbury, Barnabas Wines, Jr., and Thomas Youngs. All these men were among the early settlers of that place.

The descendants of many of these early settlers have been numerous, eminent and influential.

Not a few who trace their lineage to the first pastor are professional men—clergymen, physicians, lawyers, judges. One of his descendants was a Governor of the State of New York, and was before his election known as Col. John Youngs.

The "Wells Genealogy" shows the goodly

array of the posterity of the earliest Southold lawyer, and Clerk and Recorder of the Town.

The "Horton Genealogy" is a monument to the honor of Barnabas Horton, and a noble record of thousands of his descendants.

Large families of Dickersons and Dickinsons are descendants of Southold's Philemon Dickerson. Mahlon Dickerson, Secretary of the U. S. Navy, (who, during the autumn of 1851, erected in the cemetery of the First Church of Southold a massive marble monument to the memory of his ancestors), and his brother Philemon Dickerson, Governor of New Jersey, as well as Daniel S. Dickinson, U. S. Senator from the State of New York, sprang from the Southold settler, who came to this place by way of Salem and of Lynn, Massachusetts.

The descendants of Deacon Barnabas Wines include many eminent men, among them Gen. Wines of New Jersey, prominent in Morris County during the Revolutionary war, and the Rev. Dr. Abijah Wines, a native of Southold, who was born May 27, 1776; married a daughter of the Hon. Benjamin Giles; had two children and built his dwelling house on his farm in Newport, New Hampshire, before he commenced his preparation for Dartmouth College, from which he was graduated in 1794, and subsequently became the first Professor of Systematic Theology in the Seminary now at Bangor, Maine. To this family belongs also the late Rev. Enoch Cobb Wines, D. D., who was born in Hanover, New Jersey, Feb. 17, 1806, and became so well known as College Professor and College President, author of many volumes, especially his " Commentaries on the Laws of the Ancient Hebrews," a work which is also known in later editions as "The Hebrew Commonwealth;" and whose labors have become famous in all parts of Christendom as the foremost advocate of the age in behalf of Prison Reformation.

The following is a letter from his graceful and productive pen:

"Irvington, New York, }
Nov. 5, 1866. }
"MY DEAR BROTHER WHITAKER:
*   *   *   *   I was glad to hear from you, for I have a very pleasant recollection of our occasional interviews when a pastor at the East End." [That is, Easthampton, L. I.]
"I must own to the soft impeachment of being of the Long Island stock of Wines, and

I do not feel ashamed of my ancestry. We are of Welsh descent, a good country to be related to. I am glad you are engaged on so worthy a work, and hope it may soon appear from the press.

"I should love to visit you, and look upon the original homestead of the Wineses. Let me hear from you again.

"Truly and fraternally yours,

E. C. WINES.

"Rev. Epher Whitaker,
Southold, L. I."

The descendants of Matthias Corwin are very numerous and widely spread. "The Corwin Genealogy" indicates the names and relations of many worthy persons, among them Thomas Corwin, Congressman, Governor of Ohio, U. S. Senator, Secretary of the National Treasury, U. S. Minister to Mexico. Both of his grandparents were Southolders.

William H. Seward, Governor of the State of New York, U. S. Senator, Secretary of State of the United States during the war to suppress the great Rebellion, was a descendant of John Swezey of Southold. Hon. George W. Seward, brother of the more eminent statesman, William H. Seward, and the father of Dr. Seward, of Orange, New Jersey, and of the Rev.

S. S. Seward, of New York City, has recently
visited Southold in the interest of this relation-
ship.

Very many of the earliest comers to New
England, Long Island, and New Jersey were
a restless generation. They were rather adventurers and tradesmen than planters and settlers. But the most of the first generation of
Southold, and the most substantial part of the
people, came hither and settled here for Religion. They freely placed themselves under
the New Haven Jurisdiction. They were in
accord with the New Haven ideas and purposes. What were the motives and aims of the
New Haven planters, their first pastor, the
Rev. John Davenport, has unfolded in a mas-
terly manner. The Rev. Dr. Leonard Bacon,
the worthy pastor of the same Church, has
also faithfully set them forth in his " Historical Discourses." A paragraph from his sermon on the close of the fortieth year of his
pastorate may properly be quoted here. Of
New Haven he says: " Historically, the Town
itself, as an organized community, is a daughter of this Church. It was for the sake of
planting here a church encumbered by no human traditions, and dependent on no human

authority, that the founders of the New Haven
Colony left their homes in pleasant England,
and their trades and affairs in busy London,
and ventured their all in the enterprise of establishing here a civil commonwealth of Christian men, 'the Lord's free people;' and this is
the Church which they planted here before
their settlement had even received an English
name.   It was for the sake of gaining for their
church a place and habitation, that all this
beautiful plain, with the surrounding hills and
waters, was purchased of the savages whom
they found here.   It was for the sake of their
church that they planned this city, and reserved this central square for public uses, first of
all building here their humble temple, and
then making their graves around it."

What is thus so worthily said of New Haven is equally true of Southold.   The first
church edifice was built in the central square
on the highest ground of the settlement, freely
purchased and sacredly reserved for public
uses.   The earliest graves were made around
this public building; and these things were
done by intelligent and pious men, who deemed religion their chief interest.

Easthampton, Long Island, in the begin-

ning of its history, chose to put itself under
the Government of Connecticut rather than
unite with the Jurisdiction of New Haven;
and Southampton submitted early to a revolution, in order to exchange the New Haven
ideas and purposes for those of Connecticut;
and the pastor, the Rev. Abraham Pierson,
with a considerable number of the best of the
people, abandoned the place and settled Branford under the New Haven Jurisdiction; and
when this was merged in Connecticut, they
removed from Branford and founded Newark,
New Jersey.   But Southold effectively resisted the attempt to accomplish such a transformation here, and successfully maintained
its original character.

It was planted mainly for Religion.   This
purpose ruled the people of the settlement in
its early years as thoroughly as it controls the
people of the First Church of Southold to-day.
And if this congregation now has a right to
make its own rules, and to pursue its own religious objects, according to its own wisdom
and choice, directed by the Word of God, then
the early settlers here, in their day, had even
a more unrestricted right to the same freedom.   They left their pleasant homes, and

their dear kindred, and all the advantages
which ages of civilization afforded them in the
country of their birth; they crossed the ocean,
and plunged into the wilderness, and hid themselves in its solitudes, and toiled and suffered
to subdue its savage wilderness; they endur-
ed all the unknown and the inevitable hardships of such an enterprise, for the sake of Religion. They chose to level the forest and
plant the waste places on repulsive shores, in
order to worship and serve God according to
His word, and to promote the welfare and salvation of all those who were willing to share
their lot and were like-minded with themselves.
They did not seek to withhold nor desire to
withhold from those who were unlike-minded,
the enjoyments of the same liberty which
they claimed for themselves. The continent was large. If men supremely desired
other objects than the religion of the Bible, they could seek those objects elsewhere.
The wilderness "was all before them where to
choose." They had only to make a new plantation in the savage wild, as the Southold settlers had done. No man in this place desired
to interfere with them. But the people here
were not willing that others should come hith-

er and selfishly destroy the work for which
they themselves had crossed the ocean and
counted the cost and suffered the hardships of
planting in the wilderness a church and a commonwealth according to the word of God. If
strangers did not wish to labor for religion,
and to live according to the Divine law and
the gracious gospel of Christ, they could go
elsewhere and dig up trees' roots, as the settlers of Southold were doing here. No man
would prevent them from planting a settlement according to their own mind. And it
was only the selfish and unjust who desired to
thwart the purposes and to seize the possessions of the Christian founders of this Church
and Town ; and it is only the selfish and unjust who now wish to asperse the name of the
early settlers, because they were disposed to
maintain the same freedom and rights which
they were perfectly willing that all others
should enjoy, viz.: the liberty and the right to
plant in the wilderness among savages the
centres and settlements of a new civilization
according to their own minds and hearts, enlightened by the word of God. It is not un-
common in these days for a crowd of idlers,
thieves, vagabonds, rum-drinkers, and loose

women to swarm out of a steamer or a railroad train on a pleasant Sabbath, and pour into a quiet village near one of our great cities,
and forthwith overrun the grounds and plunder the gardens and orchards of the industrious
citizens, who have planted the orchards and cultivated the gardens for a far different purpose.
But the interlopers most violently resent and
resist any interference with their own doings.
They most stoutly insist, that no one has more
or better right to the fruits of the earth—the
common bounty of all-generous Nature—than
the children of Nature, even themselves, who
seek the supply of their wants and the gratification of their appetites in the most direct and
simple way, by taking what comes to hand.
They have very little charity for the selfishness
and exclusiveness of the Puritans who seek to
retain the advantages for which they have toiled
and suffered. It is (these robbers say) quite
too late in the day—it is altogether behind the
age—for any men or company of men to un-
dertake to retain for their own use the kindly
bounty of all-producing Nature, or to set up
claims for the sole and personal possession of
property which is fitted to promote the comfort or gratification of mankind. On these

6

principles of loafers and rowdies and thieves, and communists—on Prudhon's famous saying , *La propriete, c'est le vol*, (property is robbery)—the early settlers of New Haven and Southold, and other Puritan Plantations are greatly blamed by the bigotry of base selfishness for their efforts to defend themselves in the posession of the property and the privileges for which they suffered and toiled, and which they made valuable and productive by their own money, labor and hardships. For their resolute efforts to retain their own, they are charged with narrowness, selfishness, bigotry, sourness; and with a disposition to claim that the saints should rule the earth. The early settlers of Southold did not make this claim. Who ever did? To charge this upon them is a slander, no matter who makes the charge. It is the fruit of malice, prejudice, or ignorance, and, at this day, nearly equally blameworthy from whichever source it comes. It is like charging them with enacting and maintaining " The Blue Laws of Connecticut "—a code which never had a real, legal existence, nor any other origin than the malicious invention of the spiteful and disreputable Hugh Peters. The epithet "blue" was

applied to any one who in the reign of Charles
II. opposed the looseness, sensuality and vol-
uptuousness of the times. Thus of one's religion, it is said in Hudibras :

" 'T was Presbyterian true blue."

"That this epithet," says the New American Cyclopedia, "should find its way to the
colonies was a matter of course. It was here
applied not only to persons, but to the customs, institutions, and laws of the Puritans, by
those who wished to render the prevailing
system ridiculous. Hence, probably, a belief
with some that a distinct system of laws, known
as the Blue Laws, must somewhere have had a
local habitation. The existence of such a code
of Blue Laws is fully disproved. The only authority in its favor is Peters, who is notorious-
ly untrustworthy. The traditions upon this
subject, from which Peters framed his stories,
undoubtedly arose from the fact that the early settlers of New Haven were uncommonly
strict in their application of ' the general rules
of righteousness.' "

What the people of New Haven, and of
Southold as a part of the New Haven Jurisdiction, did maintain, was, that they had the

right to hold and rule the settlement which
they had planted in the wilderness for the
sake of religion and liberty under God; and
that it was their duty to resist every attempt
to rob them of their possessions—their bound-
en duty to thwart every design to hand them
and their plantation over to men from whose
tyranny and vices they had determined and
undertaken to escape by crossing the ocean
and planting their dwellings on unknown
shores; and by their own virtue, industry,
endurance of hardship, and devotion to God,
making the wilderness and the solitary places
glad for them, and the desert to rejoice and
blossom as the rose.   For the sake of the
freedom, and the virtue, and the piety taught
in God's word, they had crossed the sea, leaving behind them the homes of their kindred
and the graves of their fathers; they had en-
dured the rigors of an unwonted clime; they
had toiled to change the savage face of the
landscape into fruitful fields; they had suffered from storms and tempests in their lowly
hovels covered only with thatch; they had
encountered the terrors of strange and wild
beasts, and the more unnatural wildness of
savage and bloody men; they had fallen in

sorrowful numbers under the power of unusual and destructive diseases, without the remedies and alleviations of the healing art, which are desired in vain amid settlements planted in the wilderness. And yet they are blamed, and abused, and mocked, because they were unwilling to give up the fruits of such toils and hardships, and to hand over the government of their settlements to the same class of corrupters and oppressors that had caused them to brave such dangers and endure such calamities, and to escape from whose domination and wickedness they had crossed the ocean, plunging into the wilds of America in order to be free.

Faithful Christian Men ! The haters of liberty and of godliness oppressed you then ; and the haters of religion, virtue and freedom malign and revile you now. But the freedom and prosperity which we enjoy to-day, you won for us in those perilous and suffering times ; and the land which we love smiles in the light of the worth and piety which you made possible. " That the English people became Protestants is due to the Puritans." This is the testimony of George Bancroft, our great national historian ; and with equal truth

it may be said: That the United States became a free and independent nation is due
to the Puritans.   They are, under God, the authors of those principles and virtues which have
conferred upon us our religious and civil liberty.   It was in the third month of 1643, that the
Puritan Colonies of America formed their
Union and became the United Colonies of
New England.   This third month they commonly called May, for the year then began on
the twenty-fifth day of March; and on the
19th of May, 1643, the United Colonies said:
"We all came into these parts of America
with one and the same end and aim, namely,
to advance the kingdom of our Lord Jesus
Christ, and to enjoy the liberties of the gospel
in purity and peace."—Bancroft, vol 1, page
464.

It was to make sure of religious and civil
freedom and purity that the New Haven General Court for the Jurisdiction, on the 27th of
October, 1643, adopted this brief Constitution as the fundamental law of the united
plantations:

"I.   It was agreed and concluded, as a
fundamental order not to be disputed or ques-
tioned hereafter, that none shall be admitted

to be free Burgesses in any of the Plantations
within this Jurisdiction for the future, but such
Planters as are members of some or other of
the approved Churches in New England; nor
shall any but such free Burgesses have any
vote in any Elections (the six present freemen
at Milford enjoying the Liberty with the cau-
tions agreed). Nor shall any power or trust
in the ordering of any Civil Affayres be at any
time put into the hands of any other than such
church members ; though as free Planters all
have right to their Inheritance and to commerce, according to such Grants, Orders, and
Laws as shall be made concerning the same."

[For Articles II., III., IV., and V., see
Thompson's History of Long Island, and Lam-
bert's History of New Haven. The last article is this:]

" VI. The Courts shall, with all care and
diligence, provide for the maintenance of the
purity of Religion, and suppress the contrary,
according to their best light from the Word of
God, and by the advice of the Elders and
Churches in the Jurisdiction, so far as it might
concern the civill power. 2d. This Court
shall have power to make and repeal lawes,
and to require their execution while in force
in all the several plantations. 3d. To impose
an oath upon all the Magistrates, and to call
them to account for breach of the Lawes, and

to censure them according to offences; to
settle and levie rates and contribution of the
Plantations for the public service, and to hear
and determine causes, whether civill or crim-
inall; they to proceed according to the Scriptures, which is the rule of all righteous lawes
and sentences. Nothing shall pass as an act
without the consent of the majority of the
Magistrates and of the majority of the Deputies. In the Generall Court shall be and reside the supreme power of the Jurisdiction."

The New Haven Jurisdiction, with its several Plantations, continued under this Constitution until Gov. Winthrop, of Connecticut,
through his own personal influence with
Charles II., obtained the royal charter which
merged the Jurisdiction of New Haven in
the Government of Connecticut, and extended the boundaries of the latter so as to include
most of the territory of New Haven. The
officers and people of New Haven resisted
this union of the two governments for three
years, until the coming of royal commissioners
to determine boundaries caused the dwellers
in the western part of the New Haven territory to fear that they might be placed under
the authority of the Duke of York; and this
they deemed would be more intolerable than

the Government of Connecticut. Accordingly, in 1665, the opposition to the charter of
1662 generally ceased. But the Rev. Abraham Pierson and nearly all his congregation
at Branford could not endure even the Connecticut Government, and, as we have seen,
they sought a settlement elsewhere, and soon
founded Newark, New Jersey. Dr. Sprague,
in the Annals of the American Pulpit, says of
Mr. Pierson : " He was anxious that the little
colony at Southampton [on its settlement]
should become connected with New Haven,
as Southold had been [become] ; and was
dissatisfied with the agreement, in 1644, to
come under the jurisdiction of Connecticut.
He therefore removed, in 1647, with a small
part of his congregation, to Branford." " In
the contentions between the Jurisdictions of
Connecticut and New Haven from 1662 to
1665, Mr. Pierson took sides with Mr. Davenport and others against the union ; and so
strong were his feelings on this subject that,
when the event took place, he resolved to remove with his people from the colony. Ar-
rangements were accordingly made, and on
the 30th of October, 1666, he, with most of
his congregation and many prominent indi-

viduals from Guilford, New Haven and Milford, made and signed 'a plantation coven-
ant' for that purpose ; the first article of
which was 'that none should be admitted
freemen or free burgesses, but such planters
as are members of some or other of the Congregational churches, and that none but such
be chosen to magistracy, or to carry on any
part of civil judicature, or as deputies or
assistants, or to have power to vote in establishing laws, making or repealing them, or
to any chief military trust or office.' To accomplish their purpose, they removed the
next year to New Jersey and planted Newark.
The whole church, with its officers and records, abandoned their lands and homes, and
left Branford, as Trumbull says, 'almost
without an inhabitant.'" The Rev. Dr. J. F.
Stearns, in his " History of the First Church
of Newark," remarks, that they purposed " to
found a Church upon pure principles, and a
State, which, though separate in its jurisdiction,
should act in perfect harmony with the Church,
and be governed in all its procedures by the
rules of God's Holy Word." As it was in
Southold, so it was in Newark in the beginning, and indeed, according to Dr. Stearns,

" during the first seventy years, the Town transacted all the business of the Congregation; and the seventh minister, as were all his predecessors, was called to his office and had his salary fixed by a vote of the Town in the Town-Meeting." See " First Church of Newark," page 2. The Rev. John Davenport also removed from New Haven, and became the Pastor of the First Church of Boston, Massachusetts. But most of the people of the New Haven Jurisdiction, including those of Southold, believed that their liberties would be safe under the Connecticut charter, and accordingly retained their lands and remained in the homes which they had made for themselves and their children.

There is need of a clear apprehension of the main object of the early settlers of this place. The history cannot be understood without it. They did not come here chiefly to live in ease, nor to accumulate wealth, nor to acquire fame, nor even mainly to lay the foundations of a civil state or a nation. Their main object was Religion. They came here to possess and enjoy, to practice and promote the religion which they believed the word of God required. They planted a Town here for

the sake of maintaining a church uncontrolled
by men who were unwilling to obey the law
of God, made known in his own word. They
made the Bible their chief code of laws, and
the foundation and standard of all their rules
of government and conduct; and they did
this, because the religion of the Bible was
their chief concern in this life. They did not
wish to admit into their fellowship any man
whose purposes, aims, manners, morals, or be-
havior would not accord and harmonize with
the chief ends which they had in view. They
came here while their brethren of like mind
and faith, on the other side of the sea, were
writing the catechism whose first statement is
this, namely: " Man's chief end is to glorify
God and to enjoy Him forever."

They doubtless wished to serve Him in
peace and quietness, free from the contentions, oppressions and wars which were then
harrowing the souls and shedding the blood
of their fellow men in all western Europe.

For, at the very time of the settlement of
Southold, the martial forces of continental
Europe, from the remotest cape of Sweden
on the north, to the extreme limits of Spain
and Italy on the south, had already fought

through more than a score of years for and against the religious freedom and civil rights of the northern nations. These nations gained this end after a conflict which made all the western countries of Europe glow and blaze with the heat of war throughout a generation, and reduced the population of Germany from forty millions to four millions. This struggle of thirty years' continuance brought the Peace of Westphalia and secured the freedom of the Protestants precisely eight years and three days after the organization of the Southold Church.

It was in 1640 that Brazil, with other Spanish colonies, became a possession of the Netherlands, though it soon after fell into the hands of the Portuguese. Spain could extend her influence only within the limits of Italy; for there, under the popedom of Barberini, the inhabitants, having dedicated St. Peter's, now had to found the College De Propaganda Fide. Furthermore, the Pope deemed it necessary to punish Galileo for teaching the true theory of the solar system; and to condemn Jansenism, in order to quiet the Jesuits. For Jansen's "Doctrine of Augustine" was printed in 1640, and forthwith added intensity to a

7

controversy within the Papal Church which centuries seem unable to end.

The founders of Southold had grown up from their youth in a remarkable age—one most active and progressive in science and art, in war and statesmanship, in literature and religion. The chief men among them were beginning to show their beard when Shakespeare died. And it was in their time that Harvey discovered the circulation of the blood; Kepler, the wonderful relations of planetary motion; Des Cartes, the laws of refraction; Torricelli, the weight of the atmosphere; and Pascal wrote the Provincial Letters and expounded the cycloid. Then it was that Kircher invented the speaking trumpet; Gunter, his celebrated scale; Guericke set up his gigantic barometer. Then Holland's greatest writer became the champion of the free commerce of the ocean, and set forth the Rights of War and Peace. Then Sir Edward Coke wrote his Institutes of the Laws of England; Chillingworth, his Religion of Protestants a Safe Way to Salvation; Ussher, his Chronology; Bunyan, his Pilgrim's Progress; and Milton, his Reformation in England, as well as all that *can* be written for the Liberty of Unlicensed Printing. The founding of Southold was, moreover, in the times of Bochart and Selden, of Guido and Rubens, of Van Dyke and Domenicheno; but not of these, and such as these only; for it was also the times of Hampden and of Cromwell.

We sometimes boast of our own progress; but the last three hundred years have seen no quarter of a century of greater relative advancement than the years wherein the New Haven towns were under the government of the General Court for the Jurisdiction. The discoveries, inventions, and improvements, then, were as remarkable, and as important to the people, as those which we admire and praise most highly at the present day.

In England, the people had gained possession of those immense advantages which had accrued from the marvelous transformation produced by the publication and lawful use of the Bible in their own tongue; and then the half century from 1638 to 1688 saw the great uprising of liberty; the long civil war; the beheading of the King, and the overthrow of royalty; the formation of the republican commonwealth; the abolition of the hierarchy; the supremacy of Presbyterianism first, and

then of Independency in the councils of Church
and State; the prevailing fear of future insta-
bility; the restoration of monarchy; the re-es-
tablishment of prelacy; the revival of popery;
and the consequent and successful revolution
for the banishment of the papal power, and
for the security of civil and religious freedom
in England. Then English literature, advanc
ing from the immaturity and grossness of
Elizabeth's age, disclosed the great names of
Cowley and Milton, Jeremy Taylor and John
Bunyan, Lightfoot and Clarendon, Baxter and
Owen, Barrow and Tillotson, and that other
name, greater than any contemporary prelate's,
that is, John Howe. All these and more were
contemporaries of Southold's first Pastor.

And other influences were at work to affect
the character of men who were most of all
open-eyed, spiritually minded, and fond of
liberty; (and such were the first settlers of
this place); for the country, of which the
British King was a native, had taken the Cov-
enanter's Oath two years before Puritanism
struck its roots into the soil of the east end
of Long Island.

The age was full of enterprise. It was in
1640 that Englishmen gained their first foot-

hold in India; and within the lifetime of Southold, Victoria's present Empire in the East has
grown from a few acres without inhabitants
to a magnitude so vast that the Empress of
India now reigns over one fifth of the whole
population of the globe.   It is not always the
case, that

" Westward the course of empire takes its way."

For the English spirit of adventure seeks its
objects in every direction; and it has never
been greater or bolder than in the days of
Southold's early history, when the frailest
barks that ever sailed the ocean—crafts of
forty or fifty tons only, (vessels that would
now be called small sloops) ; but manned by
the most daring mariners that ever drew a sail
or turned a rudder—flitted to and fro over the
waves of the Atlantic, like clouds across the
face of heaven, while larger vessels of the
same restless nation were in every commercial city and harbor of the world.   Among
this energetic people, the spirit of discovery;
the desire of wealth; the fascination of adventure; the social freedom of a new country;
and the conflicts of religious and political par-
ties, were all active in sending traders and
adventurers, as well as religious reformers and

devotees of liberty, to this Western Continent.
England especially was a swarming hive; and
the most industrious bees that gather honey
can also sting when they are improperly dis-
turbed and hindered in their work. Tens of
thousands of these vigorous Englishmen had
already made their way across the ocean to
New England alone, before the meeting of the
Long Parliament, which convened a fortnight
after the Rev. John Youngs gathered his
Church anew in this place. It was a Parliament which proved to be perhaps the most
influential political body that ever assembled
for legislation in Great Britain.

PERIOD OF THE MINISTRY OF THE REV. JOHN YOUNGS—Continued.

1640—1672.

CHAPTER II.

It was in these circumstances, and subject to these influences, with the best motives, and pure religion for their chief object, that the first settlers of Southold laid the foundations of their Church and Town upon the Word of God.

While they were establishing their religious and political institutions, and guarding their freedom in both their Church and commonwealth with the utmost prudence, foresight and circumspection, they were also careful and busy in promoting their material interests. They had examined the soil under their feet and the sky above their heads, and chosen the site of their settlement with the greatest knowledge and skill. Unlike the planters of Southampton, they were not con-

strained to change their location at the end of
a few years. They placed the centre of their
plantation where it is in some measure shel-
tered from the winds of the icy winter by the
high bluff on the north of it, and where the
southern breezes of the summer come to it
not only from the more distant sea, without
its fogs, but also tempered by a succession of
salt water bays and streams. They planted
it where it is conveniently accessible from the
harbor putting up from the deep, broad and
beautiful Peconic Bay, and from the head of
the harbor they opened a road running nearly north and rising gently to the slightly un-
dulating plain,. eminently suitable for their
purpose, at no great distance from the water
and extending from Peconic Bay to Long Island Sound. Then, at right angles with this
road, they laid out the main street of the village, running a few points south of west.
The first lot on the south side of the main
street became the minister's house-home lot ;
the one opposite, the lawyer's. The house-
home lots of the other settlers were along
each side of the street, wherever, it would
seem, each man's lot happened to fall. But
the allotment of land was no bar to the sale

or exchange of real property among themselves. Such exchanges for convenience or
other causes were common. The street ran
almost in a right line about half a mile, and
then making an obtuse angle it continued directly south, some third of a mile, to the head
of a stream which puts up westerly from the
Town harbor ; but which, at this point, was fed
so freely by fresh springs as to afford sweet
and healthful drink for the cattle. At an early day, the street was extended eastward from
the harbor road ; and allotments of land for
tillage and of meadow for pasture in summer,
and supplies of hay for cattle in winter, were
made from time time to the freemen ; for the
people increased from year to year. In the
"Historical Sketch of Southold Town" by
Albertson Case, Esq., it is said: "Constant
accessions and additions of new settlers were
occurring in the years immediately following
the first settlement. Of these first years the
Town has no official record. There was a
book of records covering that time as appears
from the records still in existence, but no one
knows aught of it now.

"Liber A of our Town Records begins with
the date 1651, and quite naturally the record

of each man's home-lot and out lands is the
first subject embraced in the book. These
home-lots were allotted among the settlers,
and most of them are described as containing four acres more or less. Some of the
later allotments were subject to the condition
that the grantee should build upon them within three years.

"This is the way the record begins : 'Anno
Domini, 1651, Breefe records of all the inhabitants accommodations herein as follow-
eth *videl Impris*. The Reverend Mr. John
Youngs, Pastor of the Church of Christ in
Southold, aforesaid, his home-lot, with the
meadow thereunto adjoyninge, conteyning by
estimation seaven acres, more or less, bounded,' &c." This lot was on the southwest corner where the road from the harbor joined the
main street.   Just across the street and north
of the Pastor's was the house-home-lot of
William Wells, Esq.   Barnabas Horton's lots
were on the northwest and northeast corners
of the main street and Horton's lane, where
Mr. David P. Horton and Ira Hull Tuthill.
Esq., now live.   The Southold Savings Bank
and the Post Office stand on the site of John
Budd's home-lot, now the property and resi-

dence of Jonathan W. Huntting, the Post
Master and Justice of the Peace of Southold.
Richard Benjamin lived on the south side of
the street immediately west of the church-lot
and burying-ground. He was the first sexton. Capt. John Underhill's home-lot was
north of the street and on the hill west of Mr.
David T. Conklin's present residence. The
home-lot of Thomas Mapes, who was a land-
surveyor, was the site of Mr. Gilder S. Conklin's present residence, and Barnabas Wines's
home-lot was on the opposite side of the street
near the present residence of Elder Edward
Huntting. Thomas Terry's was south of
Wines's, and Philemon Dickerson's lot was
where Elder Hiram J. Terry's residence now
stands. Mr. William Y. Fithian's residence is
on the original site of Thomas Moore's lot,
and Mr. Moore's son Benjamin bought the
land and probably the present Case House at
the corner of the main street and the north
road to Greenport. Henry Case's lot included the site of Mrs. Beulah Goldsmith's present residence. On Charles Glover's original
lot now stands the residence built by J. Wickham Case, Esq., at present owned and occupied by Col. Thomas Carroll, Register of

8

Brooklyn. On the western branch of the
Town Creek, or Head of the Harbor, seems
to have lived Joseph Youngs, who was, like
Charles Glover, a mariner. The remains of
Glover's wharf were recently in existence;
and Joseph Youngs also probably built one,
for he was a wealthy shipmaster. Before his
settlement in Southold, he had been active, as
the Master of the " Love," in conveying pas-
sengers from England to America. He obtained lands at Salem, Massachusetts, in
1639; but he became one of the early settlers
of Southold.   In his maritime and mercantile
business, he was in the next generation succeeded by Col. Isaac Arnold, whose store-
house was at the Head of the Harbor. He
was a ship owner; was appointed by the Dutch
to be schout or sheriff of the Five Eastern
Towns of Long Island in 1673, but speedily
resigned; was one of the patentees of the
Town in 1676; and from that time until 1703
a judge or justice of the peace, being the
Judge of the County from 1693 to 1706. He
was in 1691 appointed one of the Judges of
Jacob Leisler, the leader of the popular party
in New York city, who was condemned and
put to death there for acting as Governor of

the Province after the Revolution in England and the flight of King James II. Col. Arnold was probably the earliest slave owner in Southold. He died November 7, 1706.

Col. John Youngs was Col. Arnold's nearest neighbor. In the second generation of this place he was the foremost man in Southold, and no other man on Long Island was so prominent. He was the eldest son of the Rev. John Youngs, Minister of the Word and first settler of Southold. Col. Youngs lived in the house which he built on the land directly north of Col. Arnold. It is now owned and occupied as his residence by Mr. Richard L. Peters, who some twenty-five years since took down the northern half of it, and made some other changes, the better to adapt it to the present mode of living; but the southern half of this noble two-story double residence stands very much as it was erected more than two hundred years ago. Col. Youngs was born about 1623, and died on the 12th of April, 1697. He early became the master of a vessel, and was active in the hostilities against the Dutch, and when he was thirty years old he and his vessel were seized at New Amsterdam (New York). Having giv-

en bonds, he was discharged the next year,
and was appointed by the Commissioners of
the United Colonies of New England to
cruise with his vessel in the North Sea (Long
Island Sound) as a part of the naval force of
the Union.   He was active in this service for
two years.   He subsequently represented
Southold at different times in the General
Court of the New Haven Jurisdiction, and
afterwards in the Legislature of the Connecticut Colony.   He was specially sent to the
latter colony in 1663 to ask aid against the
Dutch.   The next year he collected and organized a force of Southold militia to aid in the
capture of New Amsterdam (New York),
and the following year, 1665, the capture having been made, he was one of the representatives of Southold in the first Assembly at
Hempstead, under the Duke of York, when
the Duke's Laws were formally adopted for
the government of the Province of the Duke.
In 1666 he obtained from the Indians a new
deed for the territory of the Town, probably
including both larger grants and clearer de-
marcations than had been obtained in 1640.

In 1680 he became the Sheriff of Yorkshire, which included all Long Island and

Richmond and Westchester counties. Six years later, he sold to John Youngs, Jr., the beautiful property known as Calves Neck, lying between the Head of the Harbor and Dickerson's Creek, now the land owned and occupied by Col. Thomas S. Lester, on which the latter built his present residence. Col. Youngs was, at the time that he made this sale, a member of the Government Council of the Province of New York under Governor Dongan, the most enlightened and far-seeing of the Royal Governors of the Province. He was a Member of the Government Council nearly every year from 1683 to 1697.

He, as well as his nearest neighbor, Col. Arnold, was appointed by Governor Sloughter one of the Judges for the trial of Jacob Leisler. In 1693, when he was seventy years of age, he was the Colonel of a militia regiment of nine companies, including five hundred and thirty-three men. A few months before he died, he made his will, which was proved in 1698, the year after he died at seventy-five years of age.

The home-lots of many of the early settlers can now be indicated as we have seen; but on account of the loss of the earliest Records our

knowledge of the history from 1639 to 1651
is fragmentary. After this date the Records
of the Town are more full and orderly. They
give the most vivid representation of the common and faithful life of the Puritan Plantation.
They show, for instance, how, as the area of
cultivation increased, lands must be divided
by lot among the freemen and common owners; how the meets and bounds of the dividends, or divided parts of the land, must be
recorded with their situation, east, west, north,
south, between whom and in what place; how
they must be cleared and fenced in case the
timber should be cut; how each man's trees
are legally protected against the axe of every
other man; and how lots and fields for cultivation must be inclosed. For example:

"Januarie 5th 1657. The neck of land
called the calves neck lyinge on part of the
south side of the Towne shalbee layed out and
apportioned to every man his due proporcon
thereof by the first of March next; and every
inhabitant takeing upp such proporcon, shall
cleere the same, as they usually doe theire
planting land, within a yeare after the laying
out thereof under penalty of forfeiture of the
same to the Townes use."

Under date three months later is this record:
"March the last 1658. Itt was then agreed
upon at a meeting of the ffreemen that Thomas
Mapes shall lay out the Calves neck, every
man his proportion, as it shall fall by lott to
him, and for and in consideration of the same,
the said Thomas shall have his own share and
portion, next at the reere of his own lot."

The Records contain the laws determining
when woods may be fired to improve the pasture, and what privileges should be given for
building a mill on the point of Hallock's Neck,
near where Mr. Jonathan Barnes Terry built
and owns the present wharf and landing for
steamers. They show what kind of a ladder
each inhabitant must keep, to enable him
easily and rapidly to reach the top of his
thatch-covered house in case of fire; who
should be free from training, watching and
warding; how the Recorder must keep a permanent record of the levies and payments of
the Town; how the Constable must be paid
for gathering Town and Minister's rates year
by year; and how respect for rank, wealth
and other considerations must control the action of the Committees appointed from time
to time to seat the Meeting House: that is,

to assign to each person his seat in it according to rank, age, dignity, office, &c.—which continued to be done as lately at least as A. D. 1797. They also make known in what kind of meetings of the freemen the constable, selectmen, and other officers were annually elected; how any particular duties must be performed by those to whomsoever the select-men should assign them; how Sabbath-breach must be fined seven and a half bits of nine pence each; swearing, one and a half bits—a second offence, three shillings; and how at length this sliding scale made one offender's fine eight shillings; for the people of those days, though not knowing how to exclude evil entirely, yet well knew how to make vice and crime pay taxes, and not press as a heavy burden upon the shoulders of the virtuous. *It is one of the lost arts.* The early Records also disclose how slander was punished, and how the place was kept free from the bodies and odors of dead animals; though I find no law in relation to the removal of dead fish from the surface of the ground.

The Records make it plain how the Town street was maintained in good condition and other highways kept in order; how proper

regulations were made for the wharf which
John Youngs, mariner, was permitted to build
at the Head of the Harbor, near the present
residence of Mr. Francis Landon.

The following is a specimen of the local
legislation, as well as an illustration of the
record thereof:

"July 1659. It was then in like manner
ordered that from the publicacon hereof no
working cattle bee putt to foode on the com'ons
to disturbe the cowes, and for prevencon
thereof, they are to go under the hand of a
sufficient keeper, and in case any doe otherwise, they are thereby lyable to pay for one
ox so taken every tyme 12 d. The same to
continue until the'nd of Indean harvest, this
yeare and every other yeare hereafter from
the beginninge of cow keepinge till the'nd of
Indean harvest under the same penalty until
a pasture be provided to prevent the aforesaid
inconveniency."

The Records show that on the 3d of April
1679 the Town voted a site for a wind mill to
Joshua Horton, Abraham Corey and Daniel
Terry, the mill to be at Pine Neck, upon the
hill [now the property of Mr. G. Wells Phillips]
over against Peter Dickerson's house [now

the site of Elder Hiram J. Terry's dwelling].
That is, the mill was to stand where the wind
mill of Mr. Rene Villefeu stood when it burned down, a few years since.

On the 11th of March, 1667–8, there was
an adjustment of boundaries made with the
Town of Southampton. See Town Records,
Book A, page 135.

On the 13th of March, 1670–1, John Budd
sold to Isaac Arnold one-eighth of the ketch
" Thomas and John " for forty-five pounds of
current pay. Said ketch was on a voyage to
Barbadoes. The burden of the ship was rated
at forty-four tons. See Book A. page 143.
There were few men in Southold at that time
who severally had an estate worth as much as
this sloop of forty-four tons burden. Two
years later, and probably at this date, the price
of merchandise or produce often used in barter
was in Southold as follows :

Barrel of pork	£03–10–00
Barrel of beef	02–05–00
Bushel of summer wheat	00–04–06
Bushel of pease	00–03–06

The Records show some curious transactions. For instance : May 15th, 1671, Edward
Petty, son-in-law of the Minister, bequeathed

his son James, aged nine years, to Thomas Moore, Senior, and his son Joseph, four years of age, to Nathaniel Moore. Book A, page 146.

The Town Records also make known what laws were enacted for the preservation and control of boats, canoes and skiffs, as well as for pasturing cattle, sheep and goats; restraining hogs; prohibiting the sale or gift of dogs to Indians, and also rum and arms without an order from a magistrate and a full record of the whole transaction. They also show what premiums were paid for killing wolves, foxes and other kind of "varment," and that these premiums year by year made a conspicuous figure in the financial estimates and expenses of the Town.

The local enactments on record also prescribe the way in which the ratables must be presented to the proper officer by each inhabitant, and payment be made within fourteen days after the publication of the rate.

The laws of the place were evidently made by and for a pious, virtuous, prudent, industrious and forehanded community. They state how the Montauk Indians must be protected,

and how trespassers with guns must have
their guns seized and forfeited.

These specimens give an idea of the local
legislation of the place while it was under the
New Haven Jurisdiction from 1640 to 1662,
and while church members only were voters,
that is, while the Church which founded the
Town also governed it.   The earliest election
of Townsmen or Selectmen of which I have
found a record, was made on the eleventh day
of December, 1656.   At that time " William
Wells, Esq., Lieut. John Budd, Barnabas Horton, William Purrier, and Matthias Corwin
were appointed to order Town affairs according to order in that case provided until the
appointed time for a new election."

A few years later the number of the Selectmen was enlarged so as to include the Constable and eight chosen men.

How carefully they guarded their religion
and their liberty and their morals may be
seen in this record, namely :

" Januarie 19th 1654.   It was then ordered
and agreed that no inhabitant in Southold
shall lett or sett or sell wholly or in part any
of his accommodacons therein or within the
utmost bounds thereof to any person or per-

sons not being a legall townsman, without the
approbation of the ffreemen in a public meeting of theires, as also that the Towne have
the tender of the sale of house or land and a
full months space provided to return an answer."

They thought the open and unoccupied
continent broad enough for the habitation of all
disturbers, without the intrusion of unwel-
come men into the harmonious communion of
these faithful worshippers of the Lord Jesus
Christ. And who shall gainsay their right to
protect their own freedom and prosperity in
the midst of the wilderness to which they had
come for the sake of pure religion and civil
liberty? Happily, they knew their rights and
how to defend them, and so they soon made
the wilderness glad for themselves and for
their posterity, and the solitary place to show
its fruitfulness under the culture of a pious
and prosperous congregation.

The Highest Authority says, that "Man
shall not live by bread alone, but by every
word of God;" but History shows that people
and nations, even in Christian lands, rise very
slowly and gradually to the standard of life
and conduct which God's Word requires.

There is not only the depressing power of
every man's evil heart ; but there are also the
hindrances of the old, unjust and perhaps
heathen prejudices, associations and institutions.   Precedents and usages and customs,
which have no foundation in righteousness
and godliness, often obstruct the improvement of the people, and hinder the advancement of virtue and piety in human hearts and
human society.   He is a benefactor of mankind who takes these impediments out of the
way, and opens a fair field for the progress of
men in knowledge, comfort, justice, and
heartiness in the worship of God and service
of humanity.

The early settlers of this place and their
associates made an immense step in this direction when they determined that in all their
civil affairs, to which it was applicable, as well
as in their religious duties and worship, they
would be governed by the Word of God.

By making the Bible their rule of judicature, in preference to the English statutes, or
the Roman code, they gained the great advantage of a body of laws most excellent for
many other qualities, and especially for mildness and intelligibleness.   They reduced cap-

ital offences to less than twenty crimes. How
great the change is seen in this fact, that even
so recently as the time when Sir Samuel
Romilly, about 1807, began his efforts to
ameliorate the criminal laws of England, these
laws made nearly three hundred offences pun-
ishable with death; and no longer ago than
1785, the eminent moralist, William Paley,
thought it not unworthy to employ his utmost genius and skill in apologizing for this
sanguinary barbarity.

Furthermore, their adoption of the Bible
for the rule of their conduct with each other
in their civil affairs, gave them many other
benefits besides this of diminishing the number and the severity of punishments. For instance, it afforded the people generally a
knowledge of the more important laws. For
almost every man in Southold doubtless had
the Bible in his house, and read it, or heard
it read, every day; but it is not likely that
more than one of the early planters here had
a trustworthy knowledge of the statute laws
of England. They might, while living under
these statutes, commit any one of a hundred
capital offences without knowing that it was
such a crime; but with the Bible in their

hands, and heads and hearts, they were not likely to be guilty of idolatry, witchcraft, blasphemy, murder, beastiality, sodomy, adultery, incest, rape, man-stealing, false witness in a capital case, treason, incorrigible disobedience to parents, incorrigible burglary or theft, and high-handed and presumptuous profanation of the Sabbath. Most certainly they were not likely to commit these offences through ignorance of their evil character; yet it seems that these fifteen acts of wickedness and vice are the only offences which the laws of the Bible ever regarded as capital crimes. What a contrast between the Bible's fifteen and the English statutes' three hundred!

How carefully these Puritan Christians guarded the rights and promoted the welfare of men may be seen in what may be called the Bill of Rights, which they adopted for the protection of every man within the bounds of the Jurisdiction. This law declares, that " No man's life shall be taken away, no man's honor or good name shall be stained, no man's person shall be imprisoned, banished, or otherwise punished, no man shall be deprived of his wife or children, no man's goods or estate shall be taken from him under color of law or countenance of authority, unless it be by virtue or equity of some express law of this jurisdiction, established by the General Court, and sufficiently published, or for want of a law in any particular case, by the word of God. No man shall be put to death, for any offence, without the testimony of two witnesses at least, or that which is equivalent thereto."

Public Education is one of three or four main interests of the people which will probably decide the next Presidential election in the United States, and affect the history of the whole country for good or evil during many years to come. On this subject, we may all go to school to the first planters of Southold and their associates, and learn from them some wise and Christian lessons to guide our conduct in these days. Their liberal and enlightened character is held forth in the fact, that all parents and masters were required to improve such means "that all their children and apprentices, as they grow capable, might through God's blessing attain at least so much as to be able duly to read the Scriptures, and other good and profitable printed books in the English tongue, being their

native language; and, in some competent
measure, to understand the main grounds and
principles of Christian Religion necessary to
salvation; and to give a due answer to such
plain and ordinary questions as might, by
proper persons, be propounded concerning
the same." If parents and masters failed to
do this, their children and apprentices were
taken from them and committed to persons
who would be faithful to the parents' or the
masters' trust, as we do now in the case of little neglected vagrants, and in the case of children whose parents put them prematurely or
excessively into factories to perform unhealthy
tasks.

Furthermore, the founders of this place urge
their posterity to the performance of duty by
their zeal and labor for the higher and spiritual welfare and education of the people. They
had a law to this effect : The word of God, as
it is contained in the Holy Scriptures, is a
pure and precious light, by God in his free
and rich grace given to his people, to guide
and direct them in safe paths to everlasting
peace. The preaching of the same in a way
of due exposition and application, by such as
God doth furnish and send, is, through the

presence and power of the Holy Ghost, the chief ordinary means appointed of God for conversion, edification and salvation. None shall behave himself contemptuously toward the word preached, or any minister thereof, called and faithfully dispensing the same, in any congregation. Every person, according to the mind of God, shall duly resort and attend thereunto upon the Lord's days, at least, and also upon days of public fasting and thanksgiving.

Provision was also made for the organization of additional churches wherever needful, and also that the ordinances of Christ might be upheld, and a due maintenance of the ministry continued, according to the rule: " Let him that is taught in the word communicate unto him that teacheth in all good things." Should this fail to be done in a free way without rating, then every inhabitant must be assessed according to his visible estate, with due moderation, and in equal proportion with his neighbors.

Under this law an interesting case arose in the early history of the Town. On the 6th of October, 1657, the Court of Plymouth, New England, banished Humphrey Norton. He

came hither; but on account of his gross mis-
conduct in Southold he was soon after sent
away from this place to New Haven. His
trial commenced there on the 10th of March,
1657, old style—1658 new style.

The charges preferred against him were :

1. That he hath grievously and in manifold
wise traduced, slandered and reproached Mr.
Youngs, Pastor of the Church at Southold, in
his good name and the honor due to him for
his work's sake, together with his ministry
and all our ministers and ordinances.

2. That he hath endeavored to seduce the
people from their due attendance upon the
ministry and the sound doctrines of our religion settled in this colony.

3. That he hath endeavored to spread sundry heretical opinions; and that [too] under
expressions which hold forth some degree of
blasphemy, and to corrupt the minds of the
people therein.

4. That he hath endeavored to vilify or
nullify the just authority of the magistracy
and government here settled.

5. That in all these miscarriages he hath
endeavored to disturb the peace of this jurisdiction.

On these charges, he was tried and found
guilty ; sentenced to pay ten pounds ; to be

otherwise punished ; and excluded from the Jurisdiction.

The founders of Southold were far in advance of their age in respect to public records. At the present time, soldiers and sailors only can make noncupative wills. The sale of real estate cannot be made without a written deed and a record of that deed in the proper office. The sale of a large amount of personal property cannot be made without a written agreement, or the delivery of the goods by the seller to the buyer in whole or in part. But there was no requirement of this kind in England when Southold was settled. Real estate could be sold there, and any man could make his will, without a scrap of writing, as lately as the reign of Charles II. It is therefore remarkable that the Jurisdiction to which Southold freely joined itself and firmly adhered, required every bargain, sale, grant, conveyance, mortgage of any house, land, rent, or other hereditament, to be acknowledged before some court or magistrate, and recorded by the proper officer in a book kept for the purpose. We should moreover be grateful, that it was also ordered, that every birth, marriage and death should be recorded

within a month after the event; and every
man had liberty to record, in the public register of any court, any testimony given upon
oath in the same court, or before two magistrates, or any deed or evidence legally confirmed, there to remain *in perpetuam rei
memoriam.* Every inhabitant had liberty to
search and view any such public records or
registers, and to have a copy thereof, attested
by the proper officer, on paying the due fee.
It was also a law that every trial or legal pro-
ceeding should be briefly and distinctly recorded, the better to prevent after mistakes
and other inconveniences.

The Christian men who came hither into
the wilderness for Religion, had no mean and
narrow views of the nature and requirements
of religion. It was, for example, a part of
their religion to make a better distribution of
property among heirs at law than had been
previously made. When a man died without
a will, they gave at least one-third of his estate to his widow, if he left one, and two-
thirds, at most, to the children, the eldest son
taking a double portion, unless otherwise ordered by the court. When the heirs were a
widow and one child, each took a third, and

the other third was divided between them in whatever parts the court deemed best. But the scriptural causes for divorce were allowed.

The laws in respect to the neighboring heathen show a kindly and generous Christian disposition; and this, too, though the presence of the savages was a great inconvenience in many ways. No private person was allowed to purchase or truck any land of any Indian on the Island. The people in common paid the Indians for every acre of land which they occupied, and all private dealing with the red men in real estate was strictly forbidden. No one could sell implements of war to them without an order of court for a certain quantity at a specific time and on plain terms; and a full record of every such trade, with all the particulars, must be made by the magistrate who gave the leave to trade. If any one took a pawn or pledge of any Indian, as security for anything sold or lent, he could not sell the pawn without the consent of the Indian or an order of the court. In all dealings with the heathen, intoxicating drinks were put on the same footing with weapons of war. The fathers knew that rum was the leader in riot, robbery, revenge and murder.

But all their prudence and precautions did
not save them from the expense of much time
and money, in order to defend themselves, especially in times of national war between
Dutch and English. They found it needful
to require every man from sixteen to sixty
years of age to have a good serviceable gun,
always kept fit in every way for use, with all
the needful accoutrements, including a good
sword and plenty of ammunition. It was the
duty of the chief military officer of the Town
to see that every man was well furnished with
arms, and that every man trained at least six
days each year. One fourth of the whole
number were required to attend public worship fully armed every Lord's Day: and such
as could come, on Lecture Days; to be at the
meeting house at latest before the second
drum had left beating, with their arms complete, their guns ready charged, their match
for their match-lock guns, and flints ready fitted to their fire-lock guns, with shot and pow-
der for at least five shots, beside the charge
in their guns. The sentinel also, and they
that walk the round, were required to have
their matches lighted during the time of the
public worship, if their guns were to be fired

with matches and not with flint locks. During the religious service in the church building, their guns were placed in racks standing near the door. One of these racks, used here two hundred years since, has been presented to the Long Island Historical Society, and may be seen among its choicest antiquarian possessions.

It was under these and other heavy burdens, that the fathers worshipped here. It was not without faith, and fortitude, and prayer, and peril, that they prepared this place for our comfort and enjoyment. But there are some children who care very little for their parents' toils in their behalf, or even for their parents themselves. They are only eager to please and gratify their own selfishness with what their parents have earned and given them. But such meanness and baseness will be far from every noble soul; and honor should be given to the fathers, that the land which they made productive and attractive, and fruitful for the sustenance and delight of their posterity, may remain to support and bless their children for ever. If we reproach those who are ungrateful and negligent towards their natural parents, how much more should we

10

reproach ourselves unless we show gratitude
and honor towards our spiritual ancestors!

The holiest motives had impelled them to
flee from oppression, and to acquire liberty
and purity of religion for themselves and their
children, no matter at what cost of hardships
and suffering, nor how carefully they must
guard the boon.   For the sake of so great a
good, they were determined to be unceasingly
vigilant, and to close every avenue whereby
their foes might enter and gain a foothold
among them.   That their precautions and
watchfulness were judicious, and even necessary, is all too evident.   Here are, for instance,
the Private Instructions which Charles II.
gave, on the 23d of April, 1664, to Nichols,
Carr, Cartwright, and Maverick, Commissioners to subdue the Dutch, to establish boundaries, and to transact other important matters
in America.   Among other equally detestable
things, the king says: "Nobody can doubt
but that we could look upon it as the greatest blessing God Almighty can confer upon
us in this world that He would reduce all our
subjects in all our dominions to one faith and
one way of worship with us."

This statement of the monarch accords with

the general character of this voluptuous king.
For, "Sworn to maintain Protestantism, he
signed a secret treaty at Dover by which he
pledged himself to make public profession of
the Roman Catholic religion," and when he
was almost in the article of death, he declared
himself a Roman Catholic, and received extreme unction, and the last rites of the papal
church, at the hands of a proscribed priest,
who was introduced by a secret passage, in
disguise, into the king's bed-chamber. See
New American Cyclopedia, Vol. 4, p. 729.
His desire to make all his subjects fully con-
form to his own faith and worship also accords
with the St. Bartholomew's fraud and infamy
twenty months previous to his sending the
Commissioners, and many other acts of oppression at the time, whereby the people were
deprived of the services of thousands of the
best and purest Christian Ministers, who were
compelled to leave their homes and churches,
because they could not with good conscience
obey the new and wicked laws. The King,
through his Secretary of State, in his Private
Instructions to the Commissioners, speaks of
the Puritans in the New World as "persons
who separated themselves from their own

country, and the religion established, princi-
pally (if not only) that they might enjoy another way of worship, presented or declared
unto them by their own consciences." See
Brodhead's New York Documents, Vol. 3,
p. 59.

To the same class of conscientious and faithful ministers, the Rev. John Youngs undoubtedly belonged. He came here to minister
the word of God free from the control of un-
godly and despotic men, and to enjoy with
devout Christians of the same faith the liberty
of the gospel in purity and peace. He and
his people did not come without a purpose
into a country whose only inhabitants were a
few wild and roaming savages. They did
not come into such a country with the intention of oppressing, injuring, or even disturbing any human being. They came to find a
shelter from wrong, and to provide a peaceful
home for those who were like-minded with
themselves. To Mr. Youngs, as the leader
of the advance guard, his home-lot was assigned near the centre of the Town, and convenient to the church edifice, which was built
in the central square and on the highest
ground of the settlement, as well as near the

homes of the principal citizens. His possessions were ample, in comparison with those of
his neighbors and parishioners. His name,
as we have seen, with the description of his
real estate, is entered first of all in the Records of the Town.

Shortly before his death, he conveyed most
of his lands to his children. His library at
the time of his death was nearly half as valuable as all his household furniture, and one
sixth as valuable as his dwelling house and
lands.

He died February 24, 1672, of the new
style. It would seem that his venerable friend,
the good Barnabas Horton, and the saintly
Deacon Barnabas Wines, as well as his well
beloved wife, Mary, and we may suppose
some or all of his children, were with him at
or near his death. One faithful friend, his
nearest neighbor for thirty previous years,
William Wells, Esq., the Sheriff of Suffolk
county, could not be present, though he had
long held his Pastor in high regard, as the
beautiful Records which he has left us most
thoroughly attest. Mr. Wells departed this
life three months and eleven days before the
minister died. What a void was made in

Southold by the death of these two men in the same winter! Death has never made here, in so brief a time as one winter, another bereavement relatively so great.

The first Pastor's grave was made near the church edifice, and on the sunny side of it. The wall which surrounds the grave is substantial, and supports a massive horizontal slab, which bears the following inscription :

MR IOHN YONGS MINISTER OF THE WORD AND FIRST SETLER

OF THE CHVRCH OF CHRIST IN SOVTH HOVLD ON LONG ISLAND

DECEASED THE 24 OF FEBRVARY IN THE YEARE

OF OVR LORD $167\frac{1}{2}$ AND OF HIS AGE 74

HERE LIES THE MAN WHOSE DOCTRINE LIFE WELL KNOWEN

DID SHEW HE SOVGHT CRISTS HONOVR NOT HIS OWEN

IN WEAKNES SOWN IN POWER RAISD SHALL BE

BY CHRIST FROM DEATH TO LIFE ETERNALLY

The following copy of legal papers presents
a picture of the early times in Southold :
"The Inventory of pastr Youngs estate.

	£. s. d.
In wooden ware & 2 old bedsteads, & old cheist & 3 chayers 2 tables & a forme & boute & tray	02–00–00
2 kettles 2 potts hake & pot hook	03–00–00
in peuter	02–00–00
2 old beds & boulsters blankets one rugg & curtins & valancings	04–00–00
lyning & sheets & pillobans	02–10–00
5 oxen & one tame steire & one cow & 2 of 2 year old, and one half steere of one yearling	27–10–00
one horse	03–00–00
24 sheepe	12–00–00
3 small swine	02–00–00
3 chaines plow yrons & cart yrons	04–00–00
house and land	30–00–00
old books by Mr. Hubard prised at	05–00–00
	£ 97–00–00

BARNABAS WINDS
JOHN CURWIN
JOSHUA HORTON
JACOB CORE

A true copy pr me Henry Pierson, Clark."

"At a Court of Sessions held in Southold
for ye East riding of Yorkshire on Long Island by his Maj'ties authority in ye eight &
twenty yeare of ye reign of our sovereign

Lord Charles ye second by ye grace of God of great Brittaine France & Ireland King Defender of ye faith &c & in ye yeare of our Lord God 1675. Whereas an Inventory of the effects of Mr. John Yongs past: of the Church of Christ at Southold deceased was presented to ye Court as also affidavit was made by Mr. Barnabas Wines & Mr. Barnabas Horton, makeing faith yt ye sd Mr. John Yongs at or nere his death left all his estate to ye sole dispose of his wife Mris Mary Yongs also shee makeing sute to ye Court for power to administer of ye sd estate, & having put in sufficient standing security to ye Court according to law, in yt behalf: These are to certifie all whome it may concerne, yt ye sd Mris Mary Yongs, weidow & relict of him ye sd Mr. John Yongs deceased is by ye sd Court admited & confirmed to all intents & purposes Administratrix of all & singular ye goods & chattles & whatsoever estate or Invent he ye sd Mr. John Yongs died seased off, or any maner of way, rightly appertaineing to him & ye sd Mris Mary Yongs hath hereby full power as administratrix to despose of ye sd estate or any p'rcill therof, as shee hath occation and ye laws of this Government alloweth.

In ye name & by order of ye Court pr me Henry Person Clark of ye Session of ye East riding.

The Rev. John Youngs had six children by

FIRST PASTOR'S CHILDREN. 117

his first wife Anne, whose names have already
been given, namely John, Thomas, Anne,
Rachel, Mary, and Joseph. These were born
in England. He subsequently married a second wife, Mary, who was probably a widow
when he married her. She survived him,
and became by his desire the sole administratrix of his estate, as we have the legal records
to attest. Besides the six elder children, he
had a son Benjamin, who was the eldest by
his second wife, perhaps a son Samuel, and
certainly a son Christopher, his youngest son.

The Rev. John Youngs was undoubtedly a
student and teacher of the Pauline type of
theology, though he seems to have been
closely allied in disposition to that disciple
whose name he bore, and whom our Lord
specially loved. The first Southold Pastor, in
common with many Ministers and other
Christians of his age, in New England and elsewhere, greatly felt the influence of an able
writer of the previous generation, the Rev.
William Perkins, who " wrote in a much better style than was usual in his time," so that
his writings were soon translated into German,
Dutch, French, Spanish, Italian and Latin.
Our first Pastor owned and used the copy of

Perkins's Works which was conveyed by a
citizen of this place to Mr. Thomas R. Trow-
bridge, of New Haven, and presented by this
gentleman to the New Haven Colony Historical Society, for preservation among its treas-
ures.   It was printed in London, by the print-
er to the University of Cambridge, in 1616,
eleven years after the author's death.   There
is a declaration in the Records of the First
Church of Southold, made in the earlier half of
its history, that this church had been " Calvin-
istical time out of mind."   This was the system of Perkins, and doubtless it was this system
that our first Pastor taught, and herein he has
been followed by all his successors in the pastoral care of the First Church.

A few feet north of the grave of the first
Pastor is that of his eldest and most eminent
son, Col. John Youngs, and immediately
south of it is that of his grandson Benjamin,
who was for many years one of the most
prominent citizens of the Town.

Several yards westward are the graves of
two others of the earliest and most intelligent,
eminent and wealthy settlers, namely : William
Wells, Esq., and Mr. Barnabas Horton, each
marked by a massive horizontal tomb-stone.

HEERE LIES ỹ BODY OF WILLIAM

WELLS OF SOVTHHOLD GENᵗ IVSTICE OF ỹ PEACE & FIRST

Yea Here Hee Lies Who speaketh yet though dead
on Wings of Faith his soule to Heauen is fled
His Pious Deedes And charity was such
that of His praise no pen can write too much
As was His Life so was His blest Decease
Hee liud in Loue And sweetly dydn Peace

VPON LONG ISLAND WHO DEPARTE THIS LIFE NOVE 13 167 AGE 63

SHERIFFE OF NEW YORKE SHIRE

For the use of the engraving of the tomb-
stone of William Wells, Esq., the most grateful acknowlegments are due to the Rev.
Charles Wells Hayes, Rector of Saint Peter's
Church, Westfield, New York, and to his
brother, Mr. Robert P. Hayes, of Buffalo,
Auditor of the U. S. Express Company, these
gentlemen being the owners of the copyright
of the splendid volume by the former, entitled
"William Wells of Southold and his Descendants." The accomplished author of this beautiful and richly illustrated Genealogy says,
page 31 :

"In the old Burial Ground of Southold, near
the edifice (Presbyterian) which occupies the site
of the first meeting house, and not more than ten
or twelve yards from the west end of the Cemetery, is the tomb of William Wells, a substantial
structure of brick and covered with cement, and
now (1876) after the lapse of two centuries, in
perfect preservation, thanks to the reverent care
of his descendant in the sixth generation, the late
William H. Wells, of Southold. The top of the
tomb is a single slab of dark-brown stone, five
feet by two and a half, and four or five inches in
thickness, completely filled by the curious inscription, a fac-simile of which is here given, photo-
graphed from the rubbing taken by me Oct. 13,
1875."

11

Barnabas Horton was often a member of the General Court for the Jurisdiction—the Legislature of the Colony.   His tomb-stone of blue slate was imported from Mouseley, Leicestershire, England, the place of his birth.   Mr. Theodore K. Horton, of Brooklyn, when he visited Mouseley, was much interested to find the tomb-stones in the cemetery there made of the same blue slate that marks the grave and attests the godly character of his first ancestor in America.   Near the graves of Wells and Horton is the broad and heavy horizontal tomb-stone of John Conklyne, and not far away stands a large marble monument which was set up in the autumn of 1851 by the Hon. Mahlon Dickerson, of New Jersey, Secretary of the Navy in President Jackson's Cabinet, to commemorate Peter Dickerson and his sons, of Southold, from whom have descended not only Mahlon and his brother Philemon Dickerson, Governor of the State of New Jersey, but also the Hon. Daniel S. Dickinson, United States Senator from New York, as well as other conspicuous citizens of our country bearing the name of Dickerson or Dickinson.

The Clevelands came later.   See "Genealogy of Benjamin Cleveland, Chicago, 1879."

The original cemetery here might well be called God's acre, for it contained about one acre of land and was devoted to the holiest purposes. It was the site of the Meeting House for public worship, as well as the hallowed place for the burial of the dead. Used by men whose chief object, was religion, the Meeting House and the place of burial were not desecrated by their use for any of the more common and inferior purposes of the people. The cemetery, with the church edifice near its northeast corner, was the centre of the village, as well as the highest ground in the settlement. It was on the south side of the main street. There was formerly a street south of the burying ground, or central square, which was early devoted to the public uses of worship and burial. This original public grave yard is now the northwest corner of the present Church cemetery, which has been enlarged from time to time until it now includes some eight acres, about five acres having been added within the last thirty years.

Near the northeast corner of this acre the first settlers built the first church edifice. The site is now marked by a locust post standing in a depression of the soil two or three feet deep. This depression indicates the place of a subterranean cell which was made when the edifice was converted into a prison, in 1684. This conspicuous indication in the very surface of the ground pointing out the site of the first Meeting House, and of the County Prison that once stood in this place, and in use here for many years, has lost half its depth within a score of years, and is likely to disappear entirely at no distant day.

It is not known that any description of the first Church edifice is in existence. Possibly it was built of logs, hewn and squared; but most probably it was a frame structure with windows of leaden sash and diamond glass, or merely wooden shutters without any glass in the windows. In connection with the second edifice, there is mention in the Town Records of " cedar windows," which intimates that the sash of the first Meeting House was made of lead, if it contained any sash and glass at all. The first house must have been a substantial building. It was the place for all public meet- ings of every kind which Puritan Christians desired to hold in order to promote the gen- eral welfare, safety, comfort and prosperity of

the Town. All the interests of the people for
time and for eternity, for earth and heaven,
were faithfully considered in it; for it was
both their temple of worship and their tower
of defence. Their relations and duties to
their Maker, Redeemer, and Comforter, as
well as to their fellow men, were considered
and determined in this place of divine worship
and of public deliberation. It stood on the
ground that was consecrated by no words of
priestly benediction, but by the tender burial
of the dead and the hopes of the Christian resurrection, in the confident expectation that what
was sown in weakness would be raised in power;
that the mortal would in due season be immortal; and in every year, from that first year of the
fathers, when the first grave was opened to receive the first seed for the illimitable harvest, the
precious sowing has continued until the present year of grace. Here, around the spot
where the subduers of the wilderness lifted up
their prayers and praises together unto God,
now rest the old and the young, the gentle
and the strong, waiting for that day when all
that are in the graves shall hear the voice of
the Son of God, as He has most impressively
said, "and shall come forth; they that have

done good, unto the resurrection of life ; and
they that have done evil, unto the resurrection
of damnation."

The congregations that worshipped in that
Meeting House have passed beyond our sight
and observation ; but our indebtedness to
them for their example of courage, patience,
endurance, self-denial, faithfulness, and Christian devotion has not ceased. They commend
to us the religion for the sake of which they
became pilgrims and exiles from the land of
their birth and the graves of their fathers
while they sought here an abode where they
could enjoy the gospel in purity and peace ;
and while they sought, beyond their chosen
place on earth, a better country where they
could enjoy perfection and blessedness for
ever more. They rest from their labors, and
their works do follow them. Their posterity
may well emulate their virtues in faith and devotion to the honor of God and to the welfare
of mankind ; and in due season join them in
that better country to which they travelled—
the land of immortal beauty and eternal fruitfulness.

PERIOD OF THE MINISTRY OF THE REV. JOHN YOUNGS—Continued.

1640—1672.

CHAPTER III.

Among the calamities and distresses which fell to the lot of the upright man of Ur, he experienced the miseries of changes and war. These deprived him of his sons and despoiled him of his wealth. They turned into foes the very members of his own household.

The changes and war which spring from a restless, unjust and unstable government, are among the worst evils which the church has to meet and suffer in this world, while she is compelled to make her way, and, through the divine strength, to push forward her benign work, in her militant state. The First Church of Southold experienced the trials and hardships of changes and war while she was laying the foundations of the subsequent history of this Church and Town.

We shall better appreciate the advantages conferred upon us by the zeal, devotion, piety and hardships of our fathers, and by the favor of our God in protecting them, and permitting us to possess the inheritance which they prepared for us, if we properly understand those changes and wars which caused them so much uneasiness, discomfort, trouble and suffering in the early years of our history. We shall see reasons for gratefulness in their conduct, and find motives, in their supreme regard for religion, to increase our love for God's word, and our obedience to his law, and our devotion in his worship.

The planters of Southold were permitted to retain their union with the New Haven Jurisdiction for twenty-two years. Then Gov. Winthrop obtained for Connecticut the royal charter which Charles II. granted on the 30th of April, 1662. This charter extended the government of Connecticut over the territory of the New Haven Jurisdiction, including Southold. It guaranteed to the colonists the rights of English citizens; authorized the General Assembly elected by the people to make laws, to organize courts, to appoint all necessary officers for the public good, regulate military affairs, provide for the public defence, and control other public interests. Its character was so general, and it conferred such ample powers, that no change was necessary when Connecticut became, in 1776, independent of Great Britain and subject to the United States; and so the same charter continued without amendment as the constitution of the State until 1818.

The people of Southold judged that their religious and civil liberty would be safe under its protection. They accordingly recognized the authority of the government of Connecticut, which claimed Long Island as one of the "adjacent islands" mentioned in the charter. Under this claim, on the 12th of May, 1664, Connecticut appointed a committee, including the Governor and Captain John Youngs of Southold, to settle the English plantations on the Island, according to the instruction given them; and ordered them "to do their endeavors so to settle matters, that the people may be both civilly, peaceably and religiously governed in the English plantations, so as they may win the heathen to the knowledge of our Lord and Saviour Jesus Christ by their sober and religious conversation."

This Committee were active on the Island
in June 1664, and did something to accomplish
their purposes.

But in August of this year, Col. Richard
Nicholls came with a naval force and took
possession of New York, including Long Island, according to a patent which Charles II.
had given, on the 12th of March, 1664, to his
brother James, Duke of York and Albany, in
which Long Island is particularly named.
Under this grant, the Duke of York made
Richard Nicholls Governor of his province ;
and Robert Carr, George Cartwright, and
Samuel Maverick were appointed commissioners with him to take possession of the country, determine boundaries, and regulate other
affairs throughout the territory extending from
the Connecticut river to the Delaware.   These
Commissioners sent a proclamation to the inhabitants of Long Island, and promised that
all who would submit to the British King
should be protected in his laws and justice,
and peaceably enjoy whatsoever God's blessing and their honest industry had furnished
them with, and all other privileges of English
subjects.   At the close of August, the Dutch
authorities at New York surrendered to the

English, and as soon as Gov. Winthrop, of
Connecticut, saw the patent given to the Duke
of York, he informed the people of Long Isl-
and that Connecticut had no longer any
claim to the Island.   The Commissioners heard
Mr. Howell of Southampton and Capt. Youngs
of Southold give the reasons why Long Island
should be under the government of Connecticut.   But on the 30th of November, they de-
cided that Long Island must belong to the
Duke of York.   See Gov. Nicholls's letter to
Mr. Howell and Capt. Youngs.   Town Records, Book B, pp. 38, 39, 53.

On the 8th of February, 1665, the Govern-
or sent forth a proclamation ordering each of
the Towns on Long Island to elect two deputies to attend a general meeting at Hempstead, on the last day of that month, in order
to make a more formal submission to the
Duke, and to accept a new body of laws.
William Wells, Esq., and Capt. John Youngs
were chosen by the people of Southold to represent them, and to carry with them to the
Governor the following petition, namely:

These are to certifie our honored Govern-
or Coll. Richard Nicholls Esqr that according
to his command and in persuance of his sage

and sound advice the freemen of Southold in a plenary meeting made election of mstr William Wells and Capt. John Youngs and them invested with full power to conclude any cause or matter relating to all or any of the several townes comprised in the Grand Charter and to that end to waite uppon your honor at the time and place assigned by your letter of the eight of this present february 1664.

1. That there may be a law inacted that we may injoy our lands in free sockadg we and our heirs for ever.

2. That the freemen may have their choyse every yeare of all their sivell officers.

3. That every trained souldier may have his free choys of theire millitary officers yearly if they see ocatione and that we may not pay to any forttification but what may be within our selves : because we are Remott from all other townes : and that the fotte soldieres may not be injoyned to trayn without the p'cincks of the towne.

4. That we may have three courts in the towne of Southold in a year & that there may be chosen by the freemen on or two assistants to sitte in Court with those that shall be magistrates and that they may have power to try all causes and actiones except Cappitall matters and that they may tottally end all matters to the value of five pounds without any apelles.

5. That because the Gennerall Courts and

meettings are verry Remott from us that
therefore we may have some mittygatione in
our charge.

6. That not any magistrate may have any
yearly maintainance.

7. That there be not any Ratte Levy, or
Charge or mony Raised but what shallbe with
the consent of the major part of the Dep-
utyes in a Gennerall Court or metting.

On the first of March, all the deputies of
the several Towns signed an address to the
Duke, and promised, for all the people, submission to his laws, and support of his rights
and title, according to his patent from the
King.

The same meeting made a body of laws
for the government of the province, or rather accepted a code already prepared for them.
These are known as "the Duke's Laws." At
the same meeting, a shire, or county, was
formed; and after the model of Yorkshire in
England, it was divided into Ridings, East,
North, and West. The towns in the present
county of Suffolk formed the East Riding of
Yorkshire on Long Island.

The people of Southold were greatly dissatisfied with the action of their representatives, and still more so with the Duke's gov-

ernment. But Messrs. Wells and Youngs
undoubtedly did their best for the people
here, and as well as any other persons in
Southold could have done. But the early
settlers left no means unused that gave any
promise of restoring them to Connecticut,
and of releasing them from the authority and
laws of the Duke. It could not be otherwise, in view of the contrast between the
character, life and purposes of the Town, on
the one hand, and the disposition, aims, and
history of this specimen of the Stuarts, on
the other. He was the second surviving son
of Charles I. and Henrietta Maria, daughter
of Henry IV. of France. He was born in
1633, called Duke of York forthwith, and
patented as such in 1643. He was eight
years old when the civil war commenced.
He saw the first great battle of that war at
Edgehill, Oct. 23, 1642, where the forces of
the king got the advantage of their foes. He
was at the siege of Bristol the next year;
was taken prisoner at Oxford in 1646; es-
caped in 1648, and went to Holland and Flan-
ders ; in 1649, to Paris and Jersey, and thence
returned to the Netherlands. In 1651 he entered the French army; but he had to leave

France four years afterwards, and then he entered the Spanish army. In 1660, his elder brother was recalled from his exile and made King of England as Charles II. The Duke shared in the good fortune of his family, and married Anne Hyde, daughter of the Earl of Clarendon. She died in 1671, and two years afterwards, when he was forty years old, he married an Italian lady aged fifteen years. He had become a Papist while on the continent; but he did not own it until the death of his first wife. He became the head of his brother's administration in Scotland and was exceedingly cruel to the Presbyterians, who were then, as now, the most and the best of the people of that country. His brother died and he became the King in 1685. His parliament was the most slavish and his punishments the most bloody ever known in English history; but he dismissed the parliament, and undertook to overthrow the constitution, and hand over the government to the papacy. He went from bad to worse for three years. On the 10th of June, 1688, his Italian and papal wife bore a son to him. The prospect of this son's succeeding him was enough. Twenty days later, his daughter Mary and her

husband William, Prince of Orange, were invited by the real representatives of the English people, to take the throne.   William came
with 15,000 men, and James fled to France.
The next year, he passed over to Ireland and
headed a rebellion which received its death
blow at the battle of the Boyne, July, 1, 1690.
He then returned to France, said prayers to
the saints, and plotted the assassination of
William III.   He died of apoplexy in 1701.
This is the man to whose authority and laws
the people of Southold had to submit in
1665.   The Town was allowed to elect its
constable and assessors, and these officers
could make orders concerning some local interests of the people, and they were required
to appoint every year two of the assessors
to make the rate for building and repairing
the church, maintaining the minister, and sup-
porting the poor.   But the governor of the
Duke's appointment was in effect law-maker,
judge, and executive officer.   The delegates
of Southold, Southampton.and Easthampton
met in Southold in 1672 in order to unite for
the maintenance of their rights.

One instance of the Governor's arbitrary
rule was this : he gave orders, on the 19th

day of July, 1667, to the officers of Southold, and of other eastern Towns on Long Island, that one-third of the militia, which were in foot companies, should fit themselves with horses, saddles and such arms (either pistols, carbines or muskets) as they had, and be ready, at an hour's warning, to obey his orders whenever he should command them to a rendezvous. All civil and military officers were required, upon their allegiance, to promote this service strenuously and diligently.

The first Governor, however arbitrary, was a man of intelligence and wisdom; but he returned to England in 1668, and four years afterward was killed in a naval engagement in a war against Holland. He was succeeded by Col. Francis Lovelace, who soon proved to be a far less worthy governor than Col. Richard Nicholls. For Lovelace was the man who ordered one of his deputies to impose such taxes upon the people as might give them liberty for no thought but how to discharge them. In 1670, he ordered Southold and other towns on Long Island to pay taxes to build or rebuild a fort at New York, and for other purposes. The towns of Southold, Southampton and Easthampton appointed

delegates who met here in Southold to consider the matter; and after full consultation,
these Puritan towns declined to pay the taxes, unless they could have the rights and privileges of the people of New England. They
united with other towns of the Island in pro-
testing against the despotism of the Governor.
The result was, that the Governor and his
council ordered the protests to be publicly
burned.

These transactions most deeply moved the
people of Southold, who were nearly all of
them members of the church, and with whom
their purity and liberty in religion were their
chief concern. The Duke's government was un-
congenial and even irksome from the first day
of its imposition. It was steadily becoming
more uncomfortable and even hateful.

In these circumstances a new source of ag-
itation was opened. It was humiliation to
them as Englishmen; but relief to them as Puritan Christians and devoted lovers of liberty.

On the 28th of July, 1673, a Dutch fleet of
armed vessels came inside of Sandy Hook,
and two days thereafter sailed up to New
York and took possession of the place without
the firing of a gun to resist them.

They left Capt. Anthony Colve as Governor, and took away with them, on their return, Col. Francis Lovelace, whom they carried back to Europe.

Capt. Manning, the English officer who had command of the fort at the time, was afterwards tried for treachery and cowardice, pronounced guilty, and condemned to have his sword broken over his head, casting him out of the army in disgrace. Gov. Lovelace was deprived of his estate, which was given to the Duke of York.

Capt. Colve, the new Dutch Governor of the province, was a man of energy, and began forthwith to restore the Dutch authority and institutions. As soon as he had brought the city into a good condition of order and industry, he issued a proclamation, August 14, 1673, to the several towns on Long Island, requiring each of them to send two deputies to New York with full power to submit to the Dutch authority. The Towns on the West End submitted.

But Southold, Southampton and Easthampton eagerly sent their deputies to Connecticut to ask for its government and protection. Their request was referred by the General

Court to a committee, authorized to grant it,
with the concurrence of the Governments of
Massachusetts and Plymouth. The committee
took these three towns under the Connecticut
Jurisdiction, made them a county, organized a
county court, appointed judges, and commissioned other civil and military officers.

These towns adopted other means also to
accomplish their purpose, as it appears from
the following Order :

"At a Court at Whitehall, the 3d of July,
1672.

"Present—the King's Most Excellent Majesty in Council.

"Upon reading this day at the Board the
humble petition of his Majesty's subjects in
three villages at the East End of Long Island
in America, called Easthampton, Southampton, and Southold, setting forth that they
have spent much time and pains and the
greater part of their estates in settling the
trade of whale fishing in the adjacent seas,
having endeavored it above these twenty
years, but could not bring it to any perfection
till within these two or three years last past.
And it being now a hopeful trade at New
York in America, the Governor and the Dutch
there do require the petitioners to come under
their patent, and lay very heavy taxes upon

them beyond any of his Majesty's subjects in
New England, and will not permit the petitioners to have any deputies in Court, but being
chief, do impose what laws they please upon
them ; and, insulting very much over the petitioners, threaten to cut down their timber,
which is but little they have to [make] casks
for oil, although the petitioners purchased
their lands of the Lord Sterling's deputy,
above thirty years since, and have been till
now under the government and patent of Mr.
Winthrop, belonging to Connecticut patent,
which lieth far more convenient for the petitioners' assistance in the aforesaid trade.   And
therefore most humbly praying that they may
be continued under the government and patent
of Mr. Winthrop, or else that they may be a
free corporation as his Majesty's subjects for
the further encouraging them in their said
trade, otherwise they must be forced to remove, to their great undoing, and damage of
sundry merchants, to whom they stand indebted for their trade."

The King ordered the Council on Foreign
Plantations to consider this petition, and report their opinion thereon, with all convenient
speed, and also to give notice to the Commissioners of the Duke of York, that they may attend when the same shall be under considera-

tion.   See Brodhead's Documents, Vol. 3, pp. 197, 198.

The representations of this petition are touched at one point by a statemeut which Gov. Nicholls made a few years previously, when he wrote to the Duke of York in these words :

" The people of Long Island are very poor, and labor only to get bread and clothing, without hopes of ever seeing a penny of monies." See Brodhead's Documents, Vol. 3, p. 106.

On the day that Gov. Colve appointed for the Puritan Towns to submit to the Dutch authority, the Delegates from these English Towns presented to the Dutch Council the following writing :

" Jamaica, August the 14th, 1673.
" Whereas we the inhabitants of the East Riding of Long Island (namely, Southampton, Easthampton, Southold, Setauket and Huntington,) were sometimes rightly and peacefully joined with Hartford Jurisdiction to good satisfaction on both sides ; but about the year 1664 Gen. Richard Nicholls coming in the name of his Majesty's Royal Highness the Duke of York and by power subjected us to the government under which we have remained until this present time, and now by turn of God's providence, ships of force belonging to

the States of Holland have taken New York the 30th of the last month, and we having no intelligence to this day from our Governor, Francis Lovelace, Esquire, of what hath happened or what we are to do, but the General of the said Dutch force hath sent to us his declaration or summons with a serious commination therein contained, and since we understand by the post bringing the said declaration that our Governor is peaceably and respectfully entertained into the said fort and city ; we the inhabitants of the said East Riding, or our deputies for us, at a meeting this day do make these our requests as follows :

Imprimis, That if we come under the Dutch government, we desire that we may retain our ecclesiastical privileges, namely, to worship God according to our belief without any imposition.

Secondly. That we may enjoy the small matters of goods we possess, with our lands according to our purchase of the natives as it is now bounded out, without further charge of confirmation.

Thirdly. That the oath of allegiance to be imposed may bind us only while we are under Government ; but that as we shall be bound not to act against them, so also not to take up arms for them against our own nation.

Fourthly. That we may always have liberty to choose our own officers both civil and military.

Fifthly. That these five towns may be a cor-

poration of themselves to end all matters of dif-
erence between man and man, excepting only
cases concerning life, limb and banishment.

Sixthly.   That no law may be made or tax
imposed upon the people at any time but such
as shall be consented to by the deputies of
the respective towns.

Seventhly.   That we may have free trade
with the nation now in power and all others
without paying custom.

Eighthly.   In every respect to have equal
privileges with the Dutch nation.

Ninthly.   That there may be free liberty
granted the five towns abovesaid for the pro-
curing from any of the United Colonies (without molestation on either side) warps, irons
or any other necessaries for the comfortable
carrying on the whale design.

Tenthly.   That all bargains, covenants and
contracts of what nature soever stand in full
force, as they would have been had there been
no change of government.

Easthampton,	Thomas James.
Southampton,	John Jessup,
	Joseph Raynor.
Southold,	Thomas Hutchinson,
	Isaac Arnold.
Brookhaven,	Richard Woodhull,
	Andrew Miller.
Huntington,	Isaac Platt,
	Thomas Skidmore.

Deputies,"

The Records of the Dutch Council proceed:

"The Delegates from Easthampton, South-ampton, Southold, Setauket and Huntington requested an audience, and entering, delivered in their credentials with a writing in form of a petition. They further declared to submit themselves to the obedience of their High Mightinesses the Lords States-General of the United Netherlands and his Serene Highness the Prince of Orange, etc. Whereupon, the preceding petition having been read and taken into consideration, it is ordered as follows:

On the first point. They are allowed freedom of conscience in the worship of God and church discipline.

Second. They shall hold and possess all their goods and lawfully procured lands, on condition that said lands be duly recorded.

Third point regarding the oath of allegiance with liberty not to take up arms against their own nation is allowed and accorded to the petitioners.

Fourth article is in like manner granted to the petitioners: to nominate a double number for their magistrates, from which the election shall then be made here by the Governor.

Fifth. It is allowed the petitioners that the magistrates in each town shall pronounce final judgment to the value of five pounds sterling, and the Schout with the General Court of said five towns, to the sum of twenty pounds, but over these an appeal to the Governor is reserved.

Sixth. In case any of the Dutch towns shall send deputies, the same shall, in like manner, be allowed the petitioners.

On the seventh and eighth articles it is ordered, that the petitioners shall be considered and treated as all the other subjects of the Dutch nation, and be allowed to enjoy the same privileges with them.

Ninth article cannot, in this conjuncture of time, be allowed.

Tenth article. 'Tis allowed that all the foregoing particular contracts and bargains shall stand in full force."

The first noticeable feature of this business is, that the first of the deputies was a minister, the pastor of Easthampton, and that the first article of the ten included in the provisions has reference to the chief concern of these Puritan Christians, namely, religion. Their goods and lands were held secondary to this chief interest. It shows the character and objects of the men who were active here two hundred years ago; and it manifests their religious devotion in a most impressive way. It leaves no doubt as to the godly character of the men who have laid us under obligations for the inheritance which we enjoy. It plainly shows us also how broad, and liberal, and comprehensive was the nature of their religion. It was no mere matter of feeling—no narrow experience of sentiment or emotion. But it embraced all their important interests for this life as well as for that which is to come.

Ten days after these transactions, the Government of Connecticut gave the Dutch Council plain notice, that the United Colonies of New England would, through the assistance of Almighty God, maintain the liberty of the English on Long Island eastward of Oyster Bay, and keep them as a part of New England. The Dutch instantly replied to this notice with spirit and defiance, declaring that Southold and the other eastward towns belonged to the Dutch government, and would be retained by arms, should there be any need of force to retain them.

On the 8th of September, the Council elected officers for the County and for the several towns from the nominations submitted. For Schout, that is, Sheriff of the County, Isaac Arnold of Southold was chosen, and for Magistrates of this town, Thomas Moore and Thomas Hutchinson. At the same time the oath of fidelity to the Dutch government to be taken by all the inhabitants of these eastern towns was modified somewhat, with a view to make it less unacceptable to them.

The Dutch Council of War in New York were certainly very considerate and generous in their dealings with these towns. But it is not wonderful that their efforts to conciliate and keep them were in vain. They could not overcome the force of language and grateful associations.

But on the 1st of October, Gov. Colve commissioned Capt. William Knyffe and Lieut. Anthony Malypart, with the Clerk, Abraham Varlett, to call a Town meeting in each of the eastern towns, to administer unto the inhabitants thereof the oath of fidelity, and to make a true return thereof.

The business of Capt. Knyffe and his associates did not prosper. He visited all the towns, called meetings, and proposed to them the oath. But the several Towns declined to take the oath. Southold had already met, and on the 29th of September said :

"The reasons following show why we the major part of the Town of Southold aforesaid do forbear to act further than we have acted upon the summons sent us by Mr. Isaac Ar-

nold." No less than seven different reasons
are enumerated and stated, the first being
that they had understood that the Schout and
Magistrates only were to take the oath, and
the second that they would be debarred the
freedom of conscience granted in the first article of the Order made on the 24th of August.
They close their statement with these words:

"We have been left without government
about a month, which hath been prejudicial
to some and caused fear in others, we lying
open to the incursion of those who threaten
us daily with the spoiling of our goods if we
take any oath of fidelity to you ; and now you
coming amongst us, without power to settle
either civil or military government, we notwithstanding are willing to submit ourselves
to your government, (during the prevalence
of your power over us) provided you perform
those articles you first promised us, and also
establish a firm and peaceable government
among us, protecting us from the invasion of
those which daily threaten us."

Southold was followed by Southampton,
Oct. 1 ; by Easthampton, Oct. 2 ; by Setauket, Oct. 4; and by Huntington, Oct. 6—all
declining the Dutch Jurisdiction.

On the 20th of October, Gov. Colve submitted to the Council the report of Capt.

Knyffe and Lieut. Malypart, and the answers
of the Towns, and proposed whether it would
not be necessary to send a considerable force
thither to punish them as rebels. He requested the advice of the Council hereupon. After
divers debates, the majority judged that in
this conjuncture of war it was not advisable
to attack them by force of arms, and thereby
afford them and the neighboring colonies occasion to take up arms against the Dutch.
They judged it better to send a second dele-
gation.

Captain Knyffe and Ensign Vos were successful in this second visit with Setauket and
Huntington, and on the 28th of October gave
the list of names in those two towns to the
Governor, having sworn Joseph and Isaac
Platt for magistrates of Huntington and Richard Woodhull for Setauket.

On the 30th, the Governor sent hither to
the most eastward towns a most worthy delega-
tion, with instructions to dispense with the
oath, if needful, except on the part of the magistrates, Isaac Arnold, the Sheriff, having already taken it; to give them a double number
of magistrates, should they desire it; to assure
them that the instructions sent to the Schout

and magistrates should in no wise conflict with
the order formerly granted on their petition;
that they should have the right to trade with
the neighboring Colonies on as good terms as
anybody; that they shall have the nomination
of their own magistrates, and whatever they
ask in fairness; and that refusing obedience
will be their ruin. The Commissioners sent
with these instructions were the Hon. Corne-
lius Steenwyck, who was the Governor's chief
Councilor, Capt. Charles Epesteyn, and Lieut.
Charles Quirynsen. Councilor Steenwyck had
been Mayor of the city for several years under
the English Government and became Mayor
again after the restoration of the English rule.
For a time, he had been appointed Governor
of the Province in the absence of Gov. Lovelace. He was a merchant of the highest
character for honesty and worth, one of the
richest and most popular and influential men
in the colony. There was living no better
man for the Governor to appoint as the chief
of the commission; for both Dutch and English had unbounded confidence in him.

But he did not prosper in his enterprise.
He and his fellow commissioners sailed Oct.
31, in the naval sloop or snow the Zee-hond

(Seadog) about noon on Tuesday; but were thrown ashore by the current near Corlear's hook.   But they warped off and sailed to Hell-gate, where they met the flood and had to re-turn and anchor near Barent's Island.

Wednesday.   The wind blew hard from the east.   They could not sail; rowed to Barent's Island; returning, touched a rock near the *Pot;* almost upset the boat, and were in im-minent danger.

Thursday, they broke their rope and lost their anchor.

Friday, they passed the White Stone and reached Minnewit's Island.

Saturday, they sailed near Falcon's Island and met a complete hurricane.

Sunday, they reached the riff of the *Lit. tlegatt*, but lost their boat.

Monday, they pursued a sail from Pluymgat to near Silvester Island.   It proved to be a vessel conveying Capt. Winthrop and Mr. Willis, Commissioners of Connecticut.   There was a showing of commissions on each side. Mr. Silvester sent his son with a boat, and the Commissioners went on shore and passed the night with him, [on Shelter Island].

Tuesday, Nov. 7.   The Connecticut Commissioners gave a copy of their commission to the Dutch Commissioners, and requested them to proceed no further with their business ; but answer was made that the Dutch commission must be executed. Whereupon the Connecticut Commissioners hoisted the King's jack, and rowed up toward Southold in the boat belonging to Mr. Silvester's ship, with the King's jack in the stern. The Dutch commissioners immediately followed in a boat they had borrowed from Capt. Silvester, with the Prince's flag in the stern. At 2 P. M., coming near Southold, they heard the drum beat and the trumpet sounded, and saw a salute with muskets whenever the Connecticut gentleman passed by. Meanwhile, the water being low, and the tide on the turn, the boat being slowly dragged along by the sailors, the Commissioners were obliged to land. Coming nearer, they saw a troop of cavalry riding backward and forward, four of whom advanced to the Commissioners, dismounted, and courteously placed the Commissioners on their own horses ; whereupon the Commissioners ascended the heights, where they met Capt. Winthrop and Esquire Willis with a troop of twenty-six or twenty-eight men on horseback,

So they rode on towards the village.   [" The heights " are the bluff at the lower end of Bay Avenue.   The road formerly ran in a some-what curved line, and farther east than Bay Avenue, from the Main Street to the bluff, and led down to the beach eastward of the bluff, west of the present Bay Farm of Elder Stuart T. Terry].   When they reached the village, they found about sixty footmen in arms.   They went to the house of one Mr. Moore, and dismounting, they were invited to enter.   This house of Mr. Moore is the pres-ent Case house.   After a little while, Mr. Steenwyck requested that the inhabitants might be called together to hear why they had come and to hear also the commission of the Governor.   Then the Connecticut Commis-sioners answered, that the inhabitants of Southold were subjects of his Majesty of Eng-land, and had nothing to do with any orders or commission of the Dutch ; and then said to the inhabitants,: Whoever among you will not remain faithful to his Majesty of England, your lawful Lord and King, let him now speak. Not one of the inhabitants made answer.   Mr. Steenwyck replied thereupon, that they were subjects of their High Mightinesses the States-

General and his Highness the Prince of Orange, as appeared by their colors and constable's staff, by the nomination of their magistrates, presented by them to the Governor, and by the election subsequent thereon. He further requested, that the elected persons might be called. Thomas Moore appeared; but Thomas Hutchinson absented himself, and could not be found. Said Moore would not accept the election of Gov. Colve; but said he had nothing to do with it. Then Isaac Arnold, who had already been sworn in as Sheriff [he was in New York when the Dutch took the place] declared, that he had already resigned his office of Sheriff, because it was not in his power to execute that office, having been already threatened by the inhabitants that they would plunder his house. Mr. Steenwyck again asked the people, most of whom were present, if they would remain faithful to their High Mightinesses and take the oath? Not one answered; signifying plainly enough by their silence that they would not. After some further efforts, the Dutch Commissioners left the place. On leaving, some inhabitants of Southampton were present, and John Cooper, (Ruling El-

14

der of the Southampton Church), told Mr.
Steenwyck to take care and not appear with
that thing at Southampton. He repeated
this more than once; for the commissioners
had intended to go thither the next morning.
Whereupon Mr. Steenwyck asked, what he
meant by that word "thing," to which the
said John Cooper replied, "the Prince's
Flag." Then Mr. Steenwyck inquired, if he
said so of himself, or on the authority of the
inhabitants of Southampton. He answered:
"Rest satisfied that I warn you, and take care
that you come not with that Flag within range
of shot of our village."

The Connecticut commissioners asked the
Dutch what village they would visit next, and
intimated that they would be present at every
place which the Dutch commissioners should
visit.

The latter thereupon entered their boat and
rowed back toward Shelter Island, and resolved not to visit the other two villages, as they
clearly perceived that they would be unable
to effect any thing, and rather do more harm
than good.

They reached Shelter Island at ten o'clock
in the evening, and there spent the night.

The next day, Wednesday, Nov. 8th, they sailed with the ebb at noon, and passed through Plumgut, when the sun was an hour high, with a spanking breeze ; saw two sails ; spoke one, belonging to *Achter Kol*, that is, Elizabeth, New Jersey.

The next evening at 8 o'clock the commissioners reached the Fort in New York and reported to the Governor, who sent, on the 18th, a bold and vigorous letter in answer to a note received on the 5th from the Governor of Connecticut. In this letter he said :

" It is sufficiently notorious and can also appear by their requests, that the inhabitants of the East End of Long Island have submitted and declared themselves subjects of their High Mightinesses, delivering up their colors, constables' staves, making nominations for Schout, Magistrates and Secretaries ; whereupon their election also duly followed. Furthermore we have been requested by their deputies to excuse the elected Magistrates from coming hither to take the oath, but as it was necessary to send commissioners thither in order to bring the people under oath, that they may be qualified to administer the same to the magistrates in like manner, which we were pleased to grant them, and which would undoubtedly have been complied with by them, had not some evil disposed persons gone from you and dissuaded them. I am here to maintain the right of their High Mightinesses and His Serene Highness, the Prince of Orange, my Lords and Masters; therefore give little heed to your strange and threatening words, knowing to put, with God's blessing and the force entrusted unto me, such means into operation as will reduce rebels to due obedience, and to make those who uphold them in their unrighteous proceedings to alter their evil designs."

But nothing more was done through the winter to bring the people of Southold under the power of the Dutch; and with the return of Spring it became known that a treaty of peace between England and the Netherlands had been signed at Westminster on the 9th of February, restoring New York to the former in exchange for Surinam in South America, though it was not until the 10th of November that the Dutch formally yielded up the possessions on the Hudson and the neighboring waters which they had held first and last for nearly sixty years.

Thus Southold was reluctantly drawn back into subjection to the government of the Duke of York. It remained a part of his province until he became the King of England by the death of his brother, Charles II., in 1685. Then the province itself became a royal one; and it so continued until the War of Independence.

Though suffering greatly from changes and war, the early settlers laid here the foundations of liberty and religion. The lands which they had purchased from the savages, they endeavored to bring under the fruitful influence of culture; to improve the place by their own industry and piety; and to enrich it with Christian homes. They desired to possess the freedom of commerce as well as the fruits of their own toil in every field of labor, and all the privileges which they had inherited as freemen of England. But in all their aims and plans, they gave religion the chief place. This was the sacred ark in the midst of the host, whether the tribes were on the march or in the camp. They made everything else subordinate and subservient to the worship of God according to his word. Their example is a constant incitement to their posterity to emulate their faith. They lived here as pilgrims; for they desired a better country, even the heavenly. Their possessions on earth were few, and their aspirations for the riches and honors of this world restrained within narrow limits. The inventories of their goods disclose to us the property which they held and used, and the style in which they lived.

They had lands, houses, barns, fences, horses, cattle, sheep, swine, and fowls of various kinds. They used a few rude utensils for the cultivation of the soil—carts, ploughs, harrows, hoes, forks, scythes, sickles, axes, &c.

A few of the inhabitants were mechanics and artisans, such as carpenters, blacksmiths, weavers, and shoemakers. But far the greater part of them wrought directly upon the land or the water.

Within their dwellings they used tables, chairs, desks, drawers, chests, bedsteads, beds, bedding, shovels, tongs, andirons, trammels, pothooks, pots, pans, knives, wooden ware, pewter ware, especially plates and spoons, and sometimes a little earthen ware, and perhaps a few pieces of silver, as a tankard and a cup. Nearly all had guns, and some had swords and books. But stoves, tin ware, plated ware of every kind, china, porcelain, queens ware, and all kinds of fine work of the potter's art seem to have been unknown among them. So were table-cloths, and especially table-forks, which were used in Italy

as early perhaps as the settlement of Southold, but not in England until many years
thereafter. They had no carpets, and few
had any pictures, clocks, watches, musical in-
struments, or works of art for the adornment
of their homes. Some had candlesticks, but
few had lamps. Some had simple implements
for the manufacture of flax and wool into
cloth, and the families generally had scissors
and needles sufficient for making the homely
garments which they wore.

They had little food, or even condiments,
brought from beyond the Town—no coffee
nor tea. They were able to gather a scanty
supply of wild fruits; but they had little or
no other. They greatly depended upon the
mortar and pestle to prepare their grain for
cooking. Their resources, employments, implements, furniture, food, manners and habits
were unlike our own to a degree which we
cannot easily understand.

They had nets and boats for fishing and other
purposes; but how unlike those now in use!

Land was cheap; but domestic animals
were dear; and wild beasts and Indians' wolf-
ish dogs preyed upon them destructively.

In the experience of many privations and
hardships, the early settlers were social, kind-

ly and helpful to each other, bearing each
other's burdens, and so fulfilling the law of
Christ. There was much need of it; for they
were destitute of many advantages and con-
veniences which we deem indispensable.
They had the ministry of God's word for their
spiritual comfort and improvement; but for
the relief of their physical maladies in cases
of sickness and accident they could not obtain the benefit of the services of an intelligent and skillful physician. When 'death
came, they buried their dead with all serious-
ness; but they did it without funeral solemnities in order to protest against wakes, masses,
prayers for the dead, and the whole round of
superstitious rites and ceremonies which are
practiced in some places without the authority of the word of God.

The head of the household conducted the
family worship day by day, and the minister
conducted the public worship and explained
and applied the Scriptures on the Sabbath,
and on lecture, fast and thanks-giving days.

The people were in a high degree obedient
to God and just to each other. They lived at
peace among themselves, and were in a good
degree prosperous as well as contented and
thankful.

PART II.

PERIOD OF THE MINISTRY OF THE REV. JOSHUA HOBART.

1674–1717.

CHAPTER IV.

The second pastor of the First Church of Southold was the Rev. Joshua Hobart. He was the eldest son of the Rev. Peter Hobart, and a grandson of Edmund Hobart.

His grandfather came from England to Massachusetts in 1633, and settled in Charlestown; but removed two years later to Hingham, where he lived eleven years and died in 1646. From 1639 to 1642 he represented the Town of Hingham in the General Court.

He lived in England in a place where the people generally were very wicked; but he and his wife were excellent Christians, and took care to train up their children in the knowledge and practice of the true religion.

Their son Peter was born in Hingham, Norfolk county, England, near the close of

the year 1604. While he was very young,
they sent him to a grammar school near where
they lived, and in this school he advanced rapidly in his studies. They sent him afterwards
to the free school in Lynn ; and when he had
gained the needful preparation, he went to
the University of Cambridge. He pursued
his studies in the University until he became
a Bachelor of Arts. During his whole college
course, he maintained a high character as a
diligent, sober and pious person.

After his graduation, he taught a grammar
school, and lodged in the house of a clergyman of the Established Church. This rector
was not friendly to the Puritans, but he sometimes employed young Hobart, the pious
teacher, to preach for him. This continued
for a time, and then the young man returned
to the University and took his degree of Master of Arts. Thereafter, he preached in several places as he had opportunity ; and having
married an excellent wife, discreet and frugal,
like himself, he became at length a successful
minister at Haverhill, on the western border
of Suffolk county, and fifteen or twenty miles
southeast of Cambridge. He remained in
England two years after his parents, brothers

and sisters had found a new home in Massachusetts. They were urgent for him to join them in the new world. Their persuasions, and the difficulties which he experienced on account of his Puritanism, induced him to cross the ocean. He embarked in the summer of 1635, with his wife and four children. They had a long and tiresome passage, and were sick nearly all the voyage ; but at the end of it they reached Charlestown in safety, where his kindred were ready to meet them with a joyful welcome. Several churches soon invited him to become their minister ; but he preferred to make with his friends a new plantation. They did this, and called the place Hingham. Here he gathered a church and continued to be its industrious and faithful pastor for about forty years.

Soon after he came to this country his wife died. This was a great bereavement and sorrow to him. But he afterwards married another, who proved to be, like the first, a great blessing to him.

After he had been settled some time in Hingham, the church in Haverhill, whence he had come, earnestly invited him to return and become their pastor again, He felt the at-

15

tractions of the old country; but all things
being considered, he thought it best to decline
the call.

In the spring of 1670 he was very ill and
likely to die; but he had a strong desire to
live longer, especially to make some direct
efforts in behalf of the youth of his congregation, and to superintend the education of his
own younger children. God granted his desire, and he lived until January 20, 1678-9,
when he was in the seventy-fourth year of his
age. In the mean time he preached many
sermons to the young, and made other special efforts for their benefit. He had eleven
children—eight sons and three daughters.
Four of his sons became Ministers of the Gospel. Joshua was born in England, came to
this country with his parents, pursued the
college course of studies and was graduated
at Harvard College in 1650; was ordained the
Pastor of Southold, October 7, 1674, and
died February 28, 1716-7. Jeremiah was
born in England, April 6, 1631; was graduated at Harvard with his brother Joshua in
the class of 1650; was ordained at Topsfield,
Massachusetts, October 2, 1672; was dismissed September 21, 1680; was installed the

Pastor of Hempstead, Long Island, in 1683;
was dismissed thence about seventeen years
thereafter ; was installed the Pastor of Had-
dam, Connecticut, November 14, 1700; and
died March 1715, aged eighty-four years.
His wife, Elizabeth Whitney, was a descendant of Joan of Acre, daughter of Edward I. of
England, and one of the ancestors of the distinguished lawyer, Jeremiah Mason, of Boston.
[See Walworth's Mason Genealogy. 15 N.
E. Genealogical Register]. Gershom, another
son of the Rev. Peter Hobart, was born in
Hingham, Massachusetts; was graduated at
Harvard in 1667; was ordained Pastor of
Groton, Massachusetts, November 26, 1679;
and died December 19, 1707, aged sixty-two
years. Nehemiah was born in Hingham, November 21, 1648; was graduated at Harvard
in the same year as his brother Gershom. He
preached two years at Newton, Massachusetts,
and was then ordained there, December 23,
1674, and died August 25, 1712, aged sixty-
three years. Another son, Japheth, also graduated in the same class with Gershom and
Nehemiah. He was born at Hingham in
April 1647; graduated when he was twenty
years old, went two years afterward to Eng-

land as the surgeon of a ship, intending to proceed thence to the East Indies; but nothing more was ever heard of him.

The Hon. Solomon Lincoln, the historian of Hingham, Massachusetts, and President of the Webster National Bank of Boston, has generously given me the benefit of his knowledge in respect to our second pastor. He writes:

"Webster Bank,
(39 State Street and 2 Congress Street,)
Boston, June 27, 1862.

Rev. Epher Whitaker,

Dear Sir: * * * I have devoted a good deal of my time to the early history of the Town of Hingham in which I was born, and have copious notes respecting it, which I have collected with a view (perhaps not soon to be realized) of publishing a more extended history of Hingham than is contained in the small volume which I published some thirty-five years since.

I suppose I can give as much information relating to the Hobarts as can be procured elsewhere, and shall be very willing to correspond with you respecting them.

* * * I have long desired to trace the descendants of Joshua Hobart and to ascertain the precise line of the *Bishop's* ancestors.

* * * John Sloss Hobart, the Judge, was a son of Rev. Noah Hobart, the distinguished minister of Fairfield, Connecticut. Noah was a son of David, a farmer of our Hingham, and David was a son of Rev. Peter Hobart."

Subsequently Mr. Lincoln wrote me and said :

" I enclose a memorandum of some facts connected with the history of Rev. Joshua Hobart, of Southold, which may be of use to you. I have given the authority for all my statements."

The following is the memorandum mentioned above.

" Rev. Joshua Hobart, son of Rev. Peter Hobart, the first minister of Hingham, Massachusetts, was born in England, and came to this country with his father, mother and three other children in 1635, (see Hobart's Diary,) was graduated at Harvard College in 1650, (College Catalogue,) went to Barbadoes in 1655, (Manuscript of President Stiles,) and there married Margaret Vassal, daughter of William Vassal. Thence he went to London. He returned to New England in 1669, (Stiles.) His wife Margaret having deceased, he married Mary Rainsford at Boston, January 16, 1671-2, (Stiles.) He was settled in the ministry at Southold, Long Island, October 7,

1674, (American Quarterly Register, Vol. viii,
p. 336,) and died there the 'latter end of February 1716-7,' (Hobart's Diary). He survived all who were educated before him at Harvard, and it is believed all who were graduated before 1659, (Am. Quarterly Register,
Vol. viii, p. 336). Excepting Thomas Cheev-
er, it is believed that he obtained the greatest
age of any of the sons of Harvard during the
first century of its existence, (Am. Quarterly
Register, Vol. viii, p. 336). Of him President Stiles remarks : 'He was an eminent
physician, civilian and divine, and every way
a great, learned, pious man.' How many
children he had (if any) by his first wife is
uncertain. In an account of his family furnished to Rev. Dr. Stiles by Rev. Noah Hobart of Fairfield, (a nephew of Rev. Joshua,)
he says he thinks Rev. Joshua left three children by his first wife. This could not be; for
he was married to her April 16, 1656, and in a
deed dated July 18, 1657, she is called his late
wife, (Stiles). By his second wife, he had
several children, namely: 'twins born October, 1672—one died; the other was called
Aletheia [that is, Truth;] Irene [that is,
Peace,] born at Boston, April 1674; Peter
[that is, Stone,] born February 28, 1675-6 at
Southold,' and perhaps others, (Stiles). According to Rev. Noah Hobart's account, his
uncle, Rev. Joshua, died at Southold 'some
time in the winter of 1616-7,' (Stiles)."

Charles B. Moore, Esq. in his remarkably comprehensive, accurate and priceless "Indexes of Southold," says that our second pastor sailed for Barbadoes July, 16, 1655; arrived in London, July 5, 1656; and returned to New England September 5, 1659.

Mr. Moore states, in respect to the first wife, Margaret Vassal, that William Vassal, the father, was deceased, and that Nicholas Ware was acting executor. He adds:

"The dates arranged appear thus:

1656. March 3. Deed signed by *Margaret* and Mary Vassal for interest in lands in Massachusetts.

April 16. The marriage at Barbadoes, of Joshua Hobart and Margaret Vassal.

May 8. The above deeds not yet delivered in Massachusetts, and thus affected by the marriage. Power of attorney by Nicholas Ware, executor, to *Capt.* Joshua Hubbard, of Hingham, to sell property in Massachusetts.

1657. July 18. Deed of this date, signed by Joshua Hubbard, Judith Vassal and her husband, and Adams, husband of another sister, stating that J. H. signed it 'on behalf of his *late* wife.'

Enough is not shown of this deed or release to know when or where it was signed by J. H., nor whether by the Captain, under a power of attorney, or the clergyman as husband;

if the latter, probably not until after September 1659, when he returned. Prof. Stiles's MSS., which give the precise date of his return, state that he had three children by his first wife, and that she died four days after his return, which would be on the 9th of September, 1659; and if she died, as was too common in child-birth or with a young child, after a sea voyage, there is no discrepancy in having three children; nor anything very remarkable in the doctor's charge for services, or in the mere date of a deed prepared to be signed by others first, and waiting such return for her signature, then altered and signed by the husband for his late wife. (See 17 N. E. Reg., p. 58)."

This theory includes all the known facts, and therefore has the advantage of every other which fails to give each the position that seems to be its proper place.

The Rev. John Youngs died on the 24th of February 1672. The people of Southold were thus providentially bereft of pastoral oversight and care. But they were not willing to remain destitute of the ministry of God's word. On the contrary, they were prompt in their efforts to obtain a well qualified pastor. This is clearly manifest in the light of their action which is recorded as follows in the Town Records, (Book B, p. 87).

"April ye 1, 1672.

At a plenary meeting then held in Southold it was votted then and agreed that the
inhabitants wold provid themselves of an
honest godly man to performe the offis of a
minister amongst them and that they wold
allowe and pay to the said minister sixty
pounds sterling by the yeare : and yt this pay
should be Raised Ratte wise by estates as
other Rattes are Raysed uppon all the inhabitants. To which end it was agreed upon by
vote that Captain John Youngs should go in
to the bay and usse his best indevor for the
obtaining of such a man above menshoned to
live amongst us : and also agreed that he the
said John Youngs should have five pounds for
his labors and to dispach this his Trust some
tyme be twixt the date hereof and the 29 of
the next September—the which he promised
to doe."

"The bay" into which the eldest son of
the first pastor was authorized to sail, in order
to obtain a worthy, honorable, godly minister,
was of course the Massachusetts Bay, in which
colony the only college at that time in America
had been doing its work for thirty-four years.

The result of this effort to obtain a suitable
pastor appears in the Town Records under
date of May 22, 1674, (Book A, p. 159), as
follows :

"Southold 22nd May 1674.

"In a publique meeting the day & yeare abovesaid was voted & agreed by the Inhabitants of the aforenamed place, that the Revd Mr. Joshua Huberd should heave & hould for his own his Heirs & Assignes use for ever a Tract of land which said land is part of the Neck called Hallocks-neck & lyeth between the comon on the east & the land of Symon Grover, Nathan Moore and John Core senr on the west. And thirty acres of woodland lying towards the North Sea & joyning to the inclosed land of Mr. John Elton. And all the meadow lying in the Neck sometimes called by the name of Pooles neck. And a second lot of comonage.—Also the said Inhabit. have agreed & doe here promise to lay out one hundred pound upon a dwelling house for the said Rd Mr. Huburd. And have further agreed and concluded that the constable and selectmen shall see that their Ministers due from the people be brought in to him yearly.

"The Neck within named always was and is known by ye name of little Hogg-neck & not Poles neck though so worded through a mistake. And the name Pols neck is altered to ye ainciant name Little Hogg-neck by a clear voat at a Town meeting held ye 2d of April 1680. Also at the same meeting ye Town did engage to secure ye meadow.

" Memorandum.

" That in ye yeare one thousand six hundred seventy four it was agreed yt Mr. Hubart & his heirs & Assigns shall possess & enjoy for ever ye land formerly in ye possession & occupation of John Core sen : bounded northward with Nathaniel Moore, & on ye westward with ye kreek."

On the third of April 1674, (See Town Records, Book A, p. 57,) it was voted by the people that Mr. Hobart's yearly payments should end about the 25th of March, which was the beginning of the civil or legal year throughout England and the British dominions until the change from old style to new style in 1752.

On the 13th of May, 1678, it was voted at a Town Meeting that the twenty pounds promised Mr. Hobart to be added to the fourscore agreed to before he came hither, should be ratefied and paid to him as the other fourscore.

It is evident that he had a liberal settlement and support. A shilling then was worth about a dollar now, and a pound at that time nearly equivalent to a double eagle to-day. He received for his own forever, a settlement of some hundred acres of land, and a house relatively as good as a dwelling worth four thousand dollars at the present day. This would be so valuable that only a few in the parish would equal it. His salary for the first four years was eighty pounds a year. This was relatively more than three thousand dollars would be now; and, four years after his ordination, it was increased to one hundred pounds annually, equivalent to four thousand dollars a year at the present time. The Town Records contain many transcripts of his receipts for his salary, which was nearly always paid to him promptly at the end of each year during the forty-three years of his pastorate. It appears from his receipt for the year 1690, that seventy pounds and eight pence of his salary were paid by the people living west of Thomas Benedict's creek—now called Mill Creek—and twenty-nine pounds, eleven shillings and four pence were paid by those who lived east of Thomas's Creek. The town and parish at that time extended westward to Wading River, and the population had spread farther in that direction than the present limits of the town. On each side of Tom's creek there has been perhaps since that year some twenty fold increase of population; but on which side the greater relative increase, it might not be easy to determine with precision.

Closely connected with the settlement of the second pastor is a letter which he wrote to his people, April 3, 1685, namely:

"To my beloved friends and neighbors, the inhabitants of this Town, now assembled together at their Town Meeting: Salutation.

Sirs: These lines are to request you to do me the like favor that you have often done to others since I came to this place, that is, to exchange the land that you gave me at the North-sea lots for the like value of land on Pine Neck where I have already a small recompense, instead of such meadows as were promised elsewhere, but could not be obtained, which as it is situated yields me no benefit at all. So are also the other lands at North-sea lots wholly unuseful to me, the parcels being so far distant from each other. But if you would please to grant me this exchange, then I might make some advantage on Pine Neck that might satisfy me. But if you deny me, as I hope you will not, for it will make both parcels altogether unprofitable to me, which I hope none of you do design. I shall take it as a great testimony of your love and respect to me if you grant me this my desire, which if you shall do, then if you please to choose one man in behalf of the Town to join

16

with another of yourselves whom I shall desire in my behalf for to estimate and effect
this matter between us, your so doing will
oblige me who am already and still to remain
your friend and servant,

JOSHUA HOBARTT."

The people promptly granted his request,
and appointed Jonathan Horton, the youngest
son of Barnabas Horton, to act in the matter.

This exchange of land put him into the possession of all the more beautiful portion of
Pine Neck—the lower part—extending the
whole way across from Dickerson's Creek—
now Jockey Creek---to Goose Creek. This
part was the more convenient to him ; for his
dwelling was built on Hallock's Neck, northward of the cove in which Dickerson's Creek
and Young's Creek unite to flow into the Peconic Bay. Along the sand bar between this
cove and the bay, teams can pass at low tide
from Hallock's Neck to Pine Neck and return
without difficulty, while boats can pass from
one of these Necks to the other with ease at
any stage of the tide.

His dwelling was built a few rods southeast
of the site of the present dwelling of Mr.
Robert Linsley. Fragments of the materials
of the chimney, now mingled with the com-

mon soil, mark the spot ; and the old well is able at this day to supply an abundance of sweet water, as it did two hundred years ago. I have often thought, while standing on the site of this old parsonage, that it was built in the most beautiful place for a residence within the bounds of the parish. It is the central point of a scene of land and water, and fields and woods, that never loses its charm from age to age. It is not less salubrious than picturesque. The first master of the house lived in it for nearly a score of years after he had attained the proverbial three-score and ten. He retained the ownership of it for twenty-seven years, until he was more than seventy years of age, and then he sold it to the people of his charge, that it might remain a parsonage forever. This sale took place 1701, and the last payment for the property was made to Mr. Hobart two years later. It was subsequently the home of these pastors who succeeded him, the Rev. Messrs. Benjamin Woolsey, James Davenport, William Throop and John Storrs, until 1787.

There is an official list of the tax-payers of the Town made within a year of the second pastor's settlement. This gives us the names

of the chief men and two of the women who
were under his pastoral care at the beginning
of his ministry.   It is as follows :

John Paine	£119	10s
Wm. Robinson	92	10
John Greete	124	00
Caleb Curtis	106	00
Walter Jones	68	00
Giddion Yongs	141	10
Abraha. Whithere	159	00
Tho. Terry	129	10
John Tuthill	206	10
Richard Browne	370	00
Samll King	169	10
Joseph Maps	20	10
Samll Grouer	37	00
Tho. Moore Junr	186	00
Jonathan Moore	147	10
Capt. John Youngs	228	00
Mr. John Youngs Jr	148	00
Peter Simons	18	00
Mr. John Conklin	358	10
Jacob Conklin	130	00
John Cory	44	00
Richard Clark	62	00
John Booth	147	00
John Curwin	228	10
Barnabs Horton	305	00
Jonathan Horton	171	10
Richard Beniamin	247	00
Beniam. Moore	118	00

Mr. John Bud	300	00
Abraham Cory	64	10
Joshua Horton	197	00
Barnabas Wines	152	00
Isaac Ouenton	232	00
Mr. Tho. Hucisson	176	10
Jacob Cary	93	00
Tho. Reeues	137	10
John Reeues	54	10
Thomas Rider	160	10
John Franklin &		
John Wigins	176	00
Jeremy Valle	152	00
Edward Petty	95	00
Simon Grover	70	00
Nathall Moore	32	00
Mr. Thos. Moore Sr	127	00
Joseph Yongs	78	00
Isack Reeues	30	00
Samuel Youngs	72	00
Stephen Bayley	69	00
Mr. John Youngs marinr	53	00
Samll Glouer	75	10
Beniam Yongs	142	00
Christopr Yongs Sr.	120	10
Peeter Paine	58	00
Dainell Terry	126	00
Peeter Dicisson	250	10
Richard Cozens	22	00
Nathall Terry	219	00
Samll Wines	78	10

Mrs. Mary Welles	217	10
Simieon Beniam	106	00
Will Colleman	59	00
Calib Horton	282	00
Tho. Maps Jr.	99	00
Thomas Tusteene	64	00
Thomas Maps Sr	227	10
Thomas Terrill	109	00
James Reeues	244	10
Will Reeues	69	10
John Swasie Sr	200	00
John Swasie Jr	62	10
Joseph Swasie	66	00
Will Halloke	361	10
John Hallok	82	00
Richard Howell	77	00
Thomas Osman	194	00
Will Poole	114	00
Christopher Yongs Junr	56	00
John Sallmon	26	00
James Lee	10	00
Benin Horton	232	10
Sarah Yongs	72	10

On this list it is written ; "Mr. John Bud not being at home is lumpt at by ye last year accopt."

The list contains eighty-two names. To these must be added twenty-five more, for those cases in which there were more than one adult male in the family ; and then taking away two for Mrs. Wells and Mrs. Youngs, the number of full grown men appears to be one hundred and five. Most likely a few were not put into this list.

As to their possessions, let the shilling then be considered equal to the dollar now, and the Southold tax list of 1675 compares favorably with the last one made—that of 1880. Of the more wealthy men, Richard Brown is taxed for £370; William Hallock, 361 10; John Conklin, 348; Barnabas Horton, 305; John Budd, 300. Below these figures we see Caleb Horton, 282; Peter Dickerson, 250; Richard Benjamin, 247; James Reeve, 244; Benjamin Horton, 232 10; Isaac Overton, 232; John Corwin, 228 10; Capt. John Youngs, 228; Thomas Mapes, Sr., 227 10; Nathaniel Terry, 219; Mrs. Mary Wells, 217; John Tuthill, 206 10; and John Swezey, Sr., 200. Barnabas Horton and four of his sons are assessed for £1188. Ten of the Youngses are assessed for £1111 10. According to this list more of the property in the town belonged to Barnabas Horton and four of his sons in 1675 than to all the inhabitants of any other family name.

PERIOD OF THE MINISTRY OF THE REV. JOSHUA HOBART.—Continued.

1674–1717.

CHAPTER V.

Only six weeks after the ordination and settlement of the second pastor in Southold, the
people here made another earnest effort to
regain a firm and permanent union with the
Colony of Connecticut, whose charter gave
the freemen more desirable privileges and
larger liberties than any other charter granted
by an English Sovereign to an American
Colony. Accordingly, they met in Town
meeting on the 17th of November, 1674, and
took the action of which the following is the
record in Book B, p. 53 :

"Southold, November 17, 1674.
"First. We the inhabitants of sd towne being legally mett together doe unanimously re-
solve and owne, that we are at this present
time under the government of his majestys
Colony of Connetticut, and are desirous to

use all good and lawfull means so to continue.

" Secondly. We doe unanimously voat, and desire, that all spedy application be made to the government under which we are, that we may obtain their counsell and direction how we are to answer the demands of the Honored Edmund Andres Esquire Governour of New York.

" 3ly. We doe voat & determine, that some men among us be constituted and appointed a standing comitty in trust for this Town, during these transactions, to manage the affaires of concern 't to & about our lands and birth right priviledges, that may be urgent upon us eyther with Conneticutt our present government to whom under God we own our selves indebted for our protection & defence, and also with New York if we shall become under that government, this town being very remote which comitty shall have full power to act all things that may be to our better inablement for his Majesties service, & to joyne with a like comitty of South or East Hampton.

" Entd here the day & year above

" Expressed per me Benjamin Yongs Recd Mr. Joshua Hubard & Mr. Hutchson were chosen Comittee by & for said Town the day and year aforesaid."

Autograph of Benjamin Youngs in 1674.

We can very well understand the occasion
of these proceedings on the part of Mr. Hobart and his people when we call to mind that
the Dutch recovered New York on the 30th
of July, 1673, and thereupon the Towns on
the East End of Long Island asked and obtained protection from Connecticut.. But as
soon as the Dutch, on the 10th of November,
1674, surrendered New York to the English,
the Duke of York, through his Governor, required these Towns to submit themselves
again to his authority. Andros was not backward to fulfil his commission in this matter.
For this purpose, he sent hither Sylvester
Salisbury, who subsequently became high
sheriff of Yorkshire. When he reached
Southold, he called the people together, and
gave them the following notice :

" December 10, 1674. Gentlemen :
Know yee, that I am empowered by ye honored Governer of New York, to receive the
return of this place into the colony of New
Yorke, and the government thereof, pursuant
to his Majesty's royall graints to his Royall
Highnesse ye Duke of Yorke. Where upon I
doe declare to all, that I doe receive and accept of ye return and surrender of this place
from under ye Collony of Connecticut, by
whose protection they have been secured

ιrom ye Dutch invasion, unto the obedience
of his Royall Highnesse. As witness my
hand at Southold the day and year above
sayd.   SILVESTER SALISBURY."

The contest between the people of Southold and the Duke's government was an une-
qual one, and the result of it is indicated by
a paragraph in a letter of the Duke to his
governor, Major Edmund Andros, dated " St.
James's 6 Aprill 1675," as follows :

" I shall lett you know that I am well sat-
isfyed with your proceedings hitherto and yt
you are in quiet possession of yt place, but
more especially at your conduct in reducing
to obedience those 3 fractious townes at ye
East end of Long Island," &c.   [Brodhead's
Documents, Vol. III, p. 231].

The connection with New York became
more tolerable after the attainment of a Colonial Assembly, which had been long resisted
by the Duke, but which was at length gained
in 1683, when Gov. Dougan succeeded Gov.
Andros.   But the desire for union with Connecticut was not dead ; and it revived again
six years later, when the English Revolution
of 1688, the flight of the king, and the consequent dissensions in New York between Leisler and his opponents gave hope of restoration
to the New England Colony.   Therefore the

people of Southold in June, 1689, made their last vain effort for this end.

Great changes were taking place abroad on the larger field as well as in the narrow limits of Southold. London had been terribly afflicted by the great plague in 1665, and the great fire in 1666. The invading Turks, who were taking possession of the fairest portions of Europe, had received a check in Hungary in 1664, but in 1669 they conquered Candia. Among the nations of Western Europe, the English had gained some advantage over the Dutch upon the sea.

Colbert had raised France to the greatest height in military power and industrial prosperity. His financial enterprise and skill both filled the public treasury and improved the condition of the people. Spain was humbled. But the revocation of the Edict of Nantes, October 18, 1685, expelled from the country the best half-million of people that France contained. They included the most skillful artisans. England and America received many of them. They formed twenty-two Protestant French churches in London alone, and there were eleven regiments of them speedily enrolled in the English army.

England, in the year of the Rev. Joshua

Hobart's ordination and settlement, lost one of her worthiest sons, greatest statesmen, and most eminent writers, by the death of John Milton. But John Dryden and John Locke had now reached middle life, and Addison was two years old. Bunyan had come forth from his twelve years' imprisonment in Bedford jail; but it was not till 1678 that his Pilgrim's Progress came forth from the press and began a career of immortality among men.

In 1674 Jeremy Taylor had been dead seven years; but Isaac Barrow lived three years after this date, which was the very year wherein Richard Baxter published his *Method of Theology*, and he lived seventeen years thereafter.

In New England, the first generation were passing away. As they closed their eyes upon the work of their hands in the new world, they saw it prosperous and peaceful. There were more than fifty thousand people in the Puritan colonies; and the founders of these colonies, who passed into the unseen world with John Davenport and John Youngs, were gathered to their fathers, " closing a career of virtue in the placid calmness of hope, and lamenting nothing so much as that their career was finished too soon for them to witness the fullness of New England's glory." [Bancroft, Vol, II, p. 92].

But the first and second years of Mr. Hobart's pastorate were years of New England's adversity. Its prosperity was arrested by Indian wars. The savages burned villages, spoiled the frontier towns, tortured and killed all classes, and pursued the contest with the bloodiest determination for two years, until they were thoroughly overcome and King Philip was dead. The people of New England lost about 600 men, who were in the war, and as many houses, that became fuel for the flames kindled by the savages. One in twenty of the men perished, and one-twentieth of the families became houseless, while one-tenth of the property of the whole people would no more than meet the expense of the war.

Danger from the savages was always a hindrance and a burden in the early history of Southold. It was needful, in Mr. Hobart's day, as well as in previous years, to be ever vigilant. That the people maintained a careful defence appears in such records as this in 1674:

" Deacon Barnabas Wines and Richard Benjamin, Sen., are freed from training, watching and warding."

Both of these persons may have been freed on account of their office, as well as their age ; for in the same year that the second pastor was settled, the people in Town Meeting appointed a grave-digger. They elected Richard Benjamin, whose home was immediately west of the church and cemetery, his land including that now occupied by Richard Carpenter, the present Sexton of the Church, and Richard S. Sturgis, the present Constable of the parish, and extending towards the residence of Deacon Moses C. Cleveland. Mr. Benjamin was authorized to receive eighteen pence for the grave of each adult and twelve pence for that of each child. See Town Records, Book A, p. 162.

In this year Mr. John Elton was chosen Constable, and Benjamin Youngs, Recorder.

In the circumstances of the time and place, the Recorder was the most responsible civil officer of the Town. The reader will be pleased to see the fac simile of the signature of William Wells and of Benjamin Youngs. For the use of the engraving which presents the handwriting of William Wells, special and grateful acknowledgment is due to the author and copyright owners of the scholarly and elegant volume entitled "William Wells of Southold and his Descendants." It will be perceived that the dots are omitted over the " ij " in the genitive of the word Februarius, which Mr. Wells wrote " Februarij," and not February.

William Wells, Esq., had been Recorder until 1662, and from that time Richard Terry held this important office until the election of Benjamin Youngs, who filled the place from 1674 until 1687.

In the course of 1675 and 1676 it became evident, that the people here could not retain their union with Connecticut and enjoy the advantage of its liberties, the fellowship of its religion, and the protection of its charter and government. For a long period, they had declined to accept a patent confirming the title to their lands under the Duke's authority, and they continued to withhold their submission until Andros threatened to treat them as enemies who persistently refused to own the authority of their lawful sovereign. Thereupon they consented to accept a patent, and on the 31st of October, 1676, the Governor gave them one. It names as the patentees Isaac Arnold, Justice of the Peace; Captain John Youngs; Joshua Horton, Constable; and Barnabas Horton, Benjamin Youngs, Samuel Glover and Jacob Corey, Overseers of the Town. These persons received the patent for themselves and their associates, the freeholders and inhabitants of the Town. The patentees, in accepting this patent, took care to exclude from its privileges two classes of persons : first, those who were only transiently here and had no ownership in the soil—all who had rights under the patent must be owners of land. Another class that they took care to exclude consisted of all those who were freeholders but not inhabitants. They knew the evils of the proprietorship of non-residents, and they were careful to guard against them. Hence they made it sure, by the patent itself, that all who should possess the rights and privileges which it granted, must be not only freeholders, owners of land, but also dwellers in the Town.

The patentees, by their deed on the 27th of December, 1676, fulfilled the intention of the patent, and extended their rights under it to all the freeholders and inhabitants of the Town.

This patent did not avowedly disturb nor diminish the religious rights and liberties of the people. They continued to transact the business of the Church in the Town Meeting. Soon after the issue of the patent, they increased the Minister's salary to the sum of £100, and continued to assess and collect it as a part of the regular tax upon all the tax payers of the place on the same principle that the tax for public schools is now assessed and collected, the Minister being on every Sabbath and many other times the chief and most important Teacher of the people of the Town.

In preceding pages it has been said that the settlement of the Town had become permanent and so far advanced by the summer of 1640 that the Indian title was purchased at that time. This purchase did not cover the

whole territory afterwards included in the
boundaries of the Town, and hence a second
purchase was made of the Indians in 1649.
This purchase included Cutchogue, Mattituck
and Aquebogue, west of the first purchase.
Subsequently another purchase was effected
and the deed was drawn so as to include the
whole territory of the Town.   It was written
as follows :

To all people to whom this present writing
shall come, greeting.   Know ye, that whereas the
inhabitants   of   Southold their   predecessors   or
some of them, have in the right and behalf of
the said Inhabitants and Township, purchased,
procured and paid for, of the Sachems and Indians our Anncestors, all that tract of land situate,
lying and   being, at the Eastward end of Long
Island, and bounded with the River called in the
English toung the Weading Kreek, in the Indian
toung Panquaconsuk, on the West, to and with
plum Island on the East, together with the Island
called plum Island, with the Sound called the
North Sea on the North, and with a River or arme
of the sea wch runneth up between Southampton
Land and the aforesaid tract of land unto a certain
Kreek which fresh water runneth into on ye South,
called in English the Red Kreek, in Indian Toy-
onge, together with the said Kreek and meadows
belonging thereto, and running on a streight line
from the head of the aforenamed fresh water to
the head of ye Small brook that runneth into the
Kreek called panquaconsuk, as also all necks of
lands, meadows, Islands or broken pieces of meadows, rivers, Kreeks, with timber woods, and wood-

lands, fishing, fouling, hunting, and all other commodities whatsoever, unto the said Tract of land,
and Island belonging or in any wise appertaining,
as Corchaug and Mattatuck and all other Tracts
of land by what names soever named or by
what name soever called ; and whereas the
now Inhabitants of the aforenamed town of Southold, have given unto us whose names are underwritten, being the true successors of the lawful and
true Indian owners and proprietors of all the
aforesaid tract of land and Isleand, fourty yards of
Trucking cloth, or the wourth of the same, the
receipt whereof and every part of the same we
doe hereby acknowledg, and thereof acquitt and
discharg the Inhabitants their heirs successors or
assigns, and every of them by these presents.

Now these presents witnesseth, that we whose
names are under written, for the consideration
aforementioned, hath given, granted, remised and
confirmed, and doth by these presents, grant, re-
mise and confirm unto Capt. John Yongs, Barnabas Horton and Thomas Mapes, for and in behalf
of the Inhabitants and Township of Southold, and
for the use of the aforesaid Inhabitants, according
to their and every of their severall and perticular
dividends. To have and to hold to them and
their heirs forever, by virtue of the afore recited
bargain, bargains, gifts and grants of what nature
or kind soever, made with our predecessors, we
under written doe confirme all the aforenamed
Tract or tracts of land, contained within the
aforementioned bounds, as also plum Island, with
warranty against us, our heirs, or any of us or
them, or any other person or persons, claime, from
by or under us, them, or any of us or them, as
our, theirs, or any of one or their right, title or
interest, as witness our hands and seals this

seventh of December, 1665, in the Seventeenth
yeare of ye reigne of our Soveraigne Lord
Charles, by the grace of God, of England, Scotland, France and Ireland, King, defender of the
faith, &c.

Ambuscow, x his mark,   Noroumreg, x his mark,
Hammatuks, x his mark,   Washham, x his mark,
Fanckeyuon, x his mark,   Tontowish, x his mark,
Kaheummash, x his mark,   Ahambantowack,x his mark,
Sowwannous, x his mark,   Hatchedous, x his mark,
Ounsoonquat, his mark,   Hassegonhock, x his mark,
Tiscom, x his mark,   Passecoquin, x his mark,
Pancamp, x his mark,   Quaywoton, x his mark,
Matwackeom, x his mark,   Patoynamhis, x his mark,
Pimsham, x his mark,   Seequamnut, x his mark,
Kinebounch, x his mark,   Merkesump, x his mark,
Aganchu, x his mark,   Opscett, x his mark,
Antakquasen, x his mark,   Panmantanhis, x his mark,
Namlyam, x his mark   Keepcombhis, x his mark,
Webinaug, x his mark,   Odsay, x his mark,
Quahso, x his mark,   Maryack, x his mark,
Winhayten, x his mark,   Twones, x his mark,
Jamacasse, x his mark,   Tanghus, x his mark,
Cantnsquan, x his mark,   Sanysond, x his mark,
Anquapine, x his mark,   Posuassuck, x his mark,
Chackeason, x his mark,   Wegotaguati, x his mark,
            Munonex, x his mark,

Sealed and delivered in ye presence of us,
                    BENJAMIN YONGS,
                    BENONI FLINT.

The following is the text of the Town
Patent :

Edmund Andross, Esq., Seigneur of Sansmares,
Lieut. and Governour Gen'll under his Royal highnesse James, Duke of Yorke and Albany, and of
all his territory in America.

Whereas there is a certain Towne in the East
Riding of Yorke Shire, upon Long Island, com-
only called and known by the name of South

Hold, scituate, lying and being on the North side of the said Island, towards the Sound, haveing a certain Tract of land thereunto belonging, the Western bounds whereof extend to a certain river or Creeke called the Wading Creeke, in the Indian tongue Panquacunsuck, and bounded to the Eastward by Plumb Island, together with the said Island on the North with the Sound or North Sea, and on the South with an arme of ye Sea, or river which runneth up between Southampton Land and the aforesaid Tract of Land, unto a certain Creek which fresh water runneth into called in English the Red Creek, by the Indians, Toyongs, together with the Sd Creek and meadows belonging thereunto, (not contradicting the agreement made between their Towne and the Towne of Southton, after their Tryall at ye Assizes,) So running on a straight line from the head of the aforementioned fresh water, to the head of the small brook that runneth into the Creek called Panquacunsuk, including all the necks of Land and Islands within the afore described bounds and limitts, now for a confirmacon unto the present ffreeholders Inhabitants of the said Towne and precints.

Know yee that by virtue of his Ma'ties Letters Pattents and the Commission and authority unto me given by his Royal highness, I have Ratifyed, confirmed and granted, and by these presents do hereby Ratify, confirme and grant unto Isaack Arnold, Justice of the Peace, Capt. John Young, Joshua Horton, Constable, Barnabas Horton, Benjamin Young, Samuel Glover and Jacob Corey, Overseers as Patentees, for and on the behalf of themselves and their associates, the ffreeholders and Inhabitants of the Sd Towne, their heires, Successors and Assigns, all that aforementioned Tract of land, with the necks and Islands within the Sd bounds,

18

sett forth and described as afores'd, Together
with all Rivers, Lakes, waters, Quarryes, Timber,
woods, woodland, Plaines, meadows, broaken
pieces of meadows, Pastures, Marshes, ffishing,
hawking, hunting and ffowling, and all other pro-
ffits, commodities, emoluments and hereditaments
to the sd towne, tract of land and premises, within the Limmitts and Bounds aforemenconed, described, belonging, or in any wise appertaining ;
To have and to hold, all and singular the sd lands,
hereditaments and premises, with their and every
of their Appurtenances, and of every part and
parcell thereof to the Sd Patentees and their Associates, their heirs, Successors and Assigns, to
the proper use and behoofes of the said Patentees,
their Associates, their heirs, Successors and Assignes forever.   The tenure of the Sd Lands and
premises to bee according to the custome of the
manner of East Greenwich, in the County of
Kent, in England, in free and Common Soccage,
and by fealty onely, Provided, allwayes notwithstanding, That the extent of the Bounds before
recited, do no way prejudice or infringe the particular propriety of any person or persons who
have Right by Patent, or other Lawfull claime to
any part or parcell of land or Tenements within
the Limitts afores'd, onely that all the sd Lands
and Plantacons, within the sd Limitts or Bounds,
shall have relacon to Towne in Generall for the
well government thereof ; and if it shall so hap-
pen that any part or parcel of the Sd Lands, within the bounds and Limmitts aforedescribed, be not
allready Purchased of the Indyans, it may bee
purchased (as occation) according to Law.   I do
hereby likewise confirme and grant unto the Sd
Patentees and their Associates, the heires, Successors and Assignes, all the priviledges and Immuni-

tyes belonging to a Towne within this Governm't and that the place of their present habitacon and abode shall continue and retaine the name of South Hold, by which name and stile it shall be distinguished and knowne in all bargains and sales, Deeds, Records and writings, They making improvement on the Sd land, and conforming themselves according to law, and yielding and paying therefore, yearly and every year, unto his Royall highnesse use as a Quit Rent, one fatt Lamb, unto such officer or officers there in authority, as shall be empowered to receive the same. Given under my hand, and Sealed with the Seale of the Province in New York, the 31st day of October, in the 28th yeare of his Ma'ties Raigne, Anno of Domini, 1676.

E. ANDROSS.

Examined by me,
MATTHIAS NICOLLS, Sec'y.

The deed of confirmation was drawn as follows :

To all Christain people greeting. Know yee that we ye underwritten, haveing this yeare received a patent from Sr Edmond Andross, Knight, Governor for his Royall Highness the Duke of York and Albany, and dated at New-York in ye 31 day of October, in ye yeare 1676, in the behalf of our selves and of all the freeholders Inhabitants of this Towne, who are therein called Associats, wherein is contained a confirmation of all ye Lands pertaining to, and now in the possession of the respective freeholders of sd towne of Southold, with all such rights, liberties and properties, as are more at large in sd patent contained. All which freeholders, we doe fully own, admitt and declare to be our onely associats in sd patent, and no others, to whom we do hereby give full power to,

To have and to hold, possess and enjoy, to themselves, their heirs and assigns for ever, all such comon rights as are contained in sd patent, and all such perticular shars and allottments, which are now in their possessions, as fully, amply and freely, as if they and every of them had been therein named. And in further confirmation of all their properties, and shares in the premises, to such our Associats, their heirs forever, we have caused to be recorded in the page next following, all such perticular rights, tracts, and parcells of Land, as doe of right appertaine and belong unto them, their heirs and assigns in sd patent and Township. In testimony whereof, we the patentees, have hereunto affixed our hands and seals, in Southold, ye 27 day of December, in the 28 yeare of the reigne of our Soveraign Lord, Charles the 2d, of England, Scotland, France and Ireland, King, defender of the faith, &c., and in ye yeare of our Lord, 1676.

ISAAC ARNOLD,
JOHN YONGS,
JOSHUA HORTON,
BENJ. YONGS,
SAMUEL GLOVER,
JACOB COREY.

Sealed and delivered in presence of these witnesses,

JOHN GARDINER,
LION GARDINER.

The heirs of the "Freeholders and Inhabitants," who held under the foregoing Patent and Deed of Confirmation subsequently obtained the enactment of the following laws:

An Act relative to the comon and undivided Lands and meadows in Southold, in the County of Suffolk. Passed the 8th of April, 1796.

1. Whereas the proprietors of the comon and undivided Lands and meadows in Southold, by their petition to the Legislature, have requested Legislative aid, to enable them more advantageously to improve their said lands and meadows; Therefore,

Be it enacted by the people of the state of New-York, represented in Senate and Assembly : That it shall and may be lawful for the said proprietors to meet on the second Tuesday in April next, at the house of Moses Case in Southold aforesaid, and annually thereafter on the second Tuesday of April, at such a place as a majority of them shall direct, and at every such meeting the said preprietors or a majority of them who shall be present, may make such prudential rules and regulations for the better improving and managing their said common and undivided lands and meadows, as they shall judge proper ; which rules and regulations shall be entered in a book, to be provided for that purpose by a clerk to be chosen at every such meeting.

2. And be it further enacted, That the said proprietors at every such meeting, may elect three Trustees, to have the superintendance and management of their said lands and meadows, according to such rules and regulations as aforesaid to be made at such meetings. And be it further enacted, That the said trustees, or a majority of them, or the survivers of them, may sue for and recover for the use of the said proprietors, all such penalties as shall be made for the breach of the said rules and regulations, so to be made as aforesaid. Provided always that no penalty for any

one offence shall exceed the sum of three pounds.
And be it further enacted, That the said Trustees
may call a special meeting of the said proprietors,
whenever they shall judge the same to be necessary, by advertising the same at three different
meeting houses in Southold aforesaid, six days
previous to the meeting, and the proceedings of
such meeting shall be as good and valid as if they
were done at the annual stated meetings, as aforesaid.

3. And be it further enacted, That the votes of
the said proprietors at such meeting as aforesaid,
shall be counted, according to the number of rights
owned by each proprietor who shall vote at such
meeting.

An Act to amend the act, entitled " An Act
relative to the common and undivided lands and
meadows in Southold, in the County of Suffolk,"
passed April 8, 1796.   Passed November 26, 1847.

The People of the State of New-York, represented in Senate and Assembly, do enact as follows :

1. The trustees mentioned in the act entitled
" an act relative to the common and undivided
lands and meadows in Southold, in the County of
Suffolk," are authorized and empowered to prose-
cute and maintain in their own names, with the
addition of their name of office, actions of eject-
ment for the recovery of the common and undivided land in Southold ; and actions of trespass for
injuries thereto or entries thereon, and for property taken therefrom, for the use of the proprietors
of the said land.

2. No suit commenced by said trustees as aforesaid, shall be abated or discontinued by the death
of said trustees, or either of them ; but the court
in which such action is pending, shall substitute

the names of the successors upon the application of such successors of the adverse party.

3. The said Trustees whose names shall be used for the prosecution of any such suit, at the time any judgment shall be rendered therein, shall be personally liable for the payment of all costs which may be recovered against them in such suit ; and execution for the collection thereof may be issued.

Mr. Hobart was prominent in the civil and industrial interests of the people from the beginning of his ministry. He was not only the chairman of the committee with full power on the political relations of the Town to Connecticut and to New York ; but he was also executor of wills and referee in cases of disagreement as to transactions and accounts in ordinary business. He was active in the introduction and establishment of new branches of manufacture and the mechanic arts in the place. [Town Records, Book D, page 116.] He engaged more or less in the practice of medicine. He seems to have been the first person to whom the people entrusted the care of the poor, giving him due compensation therefor. See Town Record, Book D, page 11. During his pastorate the sphere of religion and of its ministry was eminently biblical and liberal. It included within its range every important interest of the people

for time and for eternity—for earth and for
heaven.   Mr. Hobart was a citizen as well as
a Christian, and every thing that concerned
the public or the private welfare of the people
concerned him.

Thus the tide of human life here flowed onward.   The rights of all were most faithfully
regarded by the people generally, and every
man was expected to keep in his own place
and to do his duty in it.   Advantage or distinction was not to be grasped without ability
and merit, nor at the expense of the public
justice or welfare, or in disregard of the rights
of any person.

This respect for the proper standing and
just claims of all persons most conspicuously
appears in the proceedings of the Town Meeting whereof the records are as follows :

"Southold, Feb. 11, 1683-4.
" Voted, that Capt. Youngs and Mr. Isaac
Arnold should have liberty to set up a pue at
the west end of the pulpit for themselves and
families."   See Town Records, Book D, page
106.

Capt. John Youngs, the eldest son of the
first Pastor, was at this time the most prominent and influential citizen in civil affairs on

Long Island; and Mr. Arnold in the same relations within the limits of Southold was second to no other than Capt. Youngs.   They
were, moreover, nearest neighbors to each
other.   It was on these considerations doubtless that the liberty was granted them to
make for themselves a place of distinction and
preference in the Meeting House.   A few
weeks after the privilege was conferred upon
them, the Town took its usual course to assign every other man his proper place and
the record thereof was made as follows:

"Southold, April 3, 1684.
"Chosen Thomas Mapes Senr Mr. Thomas
Moore Senr John Tuthill & Caleb Horton to
seate ye Inhabitance of this Town in ye meeting house."   See Town Records Book D, p.
107.

Another record of special interest in the
history of the Church is this, namely:

"Desimber ye 15th 1684.
"Ther was Then by vote Samuell Youngs
and Thomas Clarke both carpender to vewe
and apprize ye old meeting hous, in order to
make a county prison of said house, and upon
theire return they gave in they valued the
Body of the house at Thirty-five pounds."
"Ye four Seder windows left out of ye new

meeting house was sold to Jonathan Horton for three pounds in town payment." Town Records, Book D, page 108.

These dates fix the time, or at least indicate the year, when the first Meeting House was converted into a County Jail; when the second Meeting House was erected; and when the two-story part of the Horton house was added to the original edifice built soon after the settlement of the Town by Barnabas Horton. This addition was made by Jonathan Horton, youngest son and chief heir of Barnabas Horton. This house is on the north side of the street and faces south. Through the courtesy of the Messrs. Harper & Brothers an artistic picture of this house is reproduced on the opposite page, from Harpers' New Monthly Magazine, Vol. 57, No. 341, p. 715. The oldest part is the west end. It is the east end, the highest part, that was built in part for the use of the County Court, whose sessions for many years were held in this most ancient and picturesque building. The Court of Sessions for Suffolk County was holding its term at Southampton in 1683-4 when it ordered a prison to be constructed in Southold. The people here with wisdom and

thrift turned their old fortification-like Meeting House into the required prison, and erected a new edifice more appropriate for their public worship and other uses in less warlike times. See Town Records, Book D, p. 219. They probably built this on the north side of the street, nearly opposite the first one, which had now become a jail. The Third meeting House, which immediately preceded the present one, stood on the north side of the street and opposite the site of the first.

For a few years after the building of the new meeting house, in 1684, no events of importance known to us marked the peaceful history of the pastor and his flock in their Island home. There were, of course, the ceaseless changes of this transient life—one generation was passing away and another generation coming. Some were seeking new homes in other places ; and others were fixing their habitations here. Some of these changes are indicated by a comparison of the tax-lists of 1675 and 1683.

The list of 1683 contains ninety-eight names, as follows :

| Mr. John Budd | £350 00 s |
| Jeremiah Vail Sr. | 74 00 |

19

John Paine Jr	40	00
Jasper Griffing	111	00
Henry Case	35	00
Lot Johnson	19	00
Simon Grover	73	00
Nathaniel Moore	46	00
Thomas Moore Sr	49	00
Joseph Youngs	98	00
Samuel Youngs	84	00
Peter Paine	56	00
Christopher Youngs	80	00
Stephen Bailey	103	00
John Bailey	18	00
John Youngs, mariner	58	00
Benjamin Youngs	123	00
John Salmon	41	00
Mr. John Booth	131	00
John Carwine	131	06
Thomas Prickman	42	00
Jonathan Horton	440	13
Richard Benjamin	133	00
Benjamin Moore	80	10
Jeremiah Vail Jr	103	00
John Hallock	80	00
Abraham Corey	76	00
Ann Elton	77	00
Joshua Horton	173	00
Isaac Oventon	100	10
Barnabas Wines	122	00
Jacob Corey	92	00
Theophilus Case	109	00

The widow Terry	97	00
John Reeve	76	00
Daniel Terry	141	00
Peter Dickerson	121	00
Thomas Dickerson	83	00
Joseph Reeve	65	00
Nathaniel Terry	73	00
William Wells	85	00
Josiah Wells	81	00
Samuel Wines	82	00
Simeon Benjamin	117	00
Gershom Terry	84	00
John Goldsmith	121	00
Thomas Mapes Jr	128	00
Caleb Horton	350	00
Benjamin Horton	267	00
William Coleman	78	00
William Reeve	100	00
Thomas Tuston	66	00
Theophilus Curwin	84	00
Thomas Mapes Sr	244	00
James Reeve	228	00
Thomas Terrill	105	00
Peter Aldrich	40	00
Thomas Osman	228	00
William Hallock	236	00
Thomas Hallock	81	00
John Swazey	202	00
Joseph Swazey	99	00
John Franklin	33	00
Thomas Rider	166	00
Jacob Conklin	101	00

John Hopson	83	00
John Conklin	321	00
William Hopkins	46	00
John Racket	57	00
Jonathan Moore	202	00
John Youngs Jr	225	00
Christopher Youngs	44	00
Timothy Martin	57	00
John Wiggins	68	00
Thomas Moore Jr	137	00
Richard Brown Sr ⎫		
Richard Brown Jr ⎬	386	00
Jonathan Brown ⎭		
John Tuthill Sr	239	00
John Tuthill Jr	99	00
Samuel King	150	00
Abraham Whittier	180	00
Thomas Terry	139	00
Gideon Youngs	173	00
John Paine Sr	94	00
Edward Petty	62	00
John Loring	76	00
Samuel Glover	104	00
Caleb Curtis	108	00
Cornelius Paine	81	00
Richard Howell	98	00
Thomas Booth	45	00
John Liman	18	00
Ebine. Davis	30	00
Richard Edgecomb	18	00
John Booth Jr	18	00
Jonathan Reeve	30	00

On the list of 1675 are some twenty names which do not appear on that of 1683, namely:

Richard Clark	Joseph Mapes
John Corey	William Poole
Richard Cozens	William Robinson
John Greete	Isaac Reeve
Samuel Grover	Thomas Reeve
Barnabas Horton	John Swezey Jr
John Halloch	Peter Simons
Thomas Hutchinson	Mrs. Mary Wells
Walter Jones	Capt. John Youngs
James Lee	Sarah Youngs
Thomas Moore Jr	

On the other hand, the list of 1683 contains the following names which are not found in " the estimation" officially attested eight years earlier, namely:

Peter Aldridge	Lot Johnson
John Bailey	John Loring
Richard Brown Jr	John Liman
Jonathan Brown	Timothy Martin
Thomas Booth	Thomas Moore Jr
John Booth Jr	John Osman
Henry Case	Thomas Prickman
Theophilus Case	Cornelius Paine
Theophilus Corwin	Joseph Reeve
Thomas Dickerson	Jonathan Reeve
Ebenezer Davis	John Rackett
Ann Elton	Joseph Swezey
Richard Edgecomb	The widow Terry

Jasper Griffing	Gershom Terry
John Goldsmith	John Tuthill Jr
Thomas Hallock	Jeremiah Vail Jr
John Hopson	William Wells
William Hopkins	Josiah Wells

Thus it seems that in the course of eight years the names of twenty-one tax-payers had disappeared from the list and in the same time thirty-six had been added. These facts make it evident, that in the first part of the second pastor's ministry, his people were increasing at the rate of two families or tax payers a year.

These lists of two hundred years ago indicate also that the richer men of the seventeenth century, to a greater extent than the poorer ones, have sent down their family names and perpetuated them in the old Town until the present day; for instance, those of Benjamin, Brown, Budd, Conklin, Corwin, Dickerson, Hallock, Horton, Mapes, Overton, Reeve, Swezey, Terry, Tuthill, Wells, and Youngs, nearly all remain here; and these are all that are assessed for more than two hundred pounds each in the earliest list; while the names of Cozens, Coleman, Lee and Tusten, together with Johnson, Prickman,

Hopson, Hopkins, Martin, Loring, Liman, Edgecomb, have, I believe, utterly vanished away; and the estates of these latter were estimated at comparatively small amounts.

In 1697, the people, in their Town Meeting, appointed four men to agree with John Herbert upon a price for his house-home-lot, being two acres in Calves' neck, and two lots of meadow in Cutchogue, and two lots of undivided commonage. They agreed for seventy-five pounds in silver. And on the 10th of November, 1697, it was ordered, that this house-home-lot land in Calves' neck be and remain to be for such minister or ministers as may be chosen and accepted by the major part of the inhabitants for the future.

This John Herbert was the son of John Herbert, a shoemaker from Northampton, England, who probably came to America in 1635, when he was twenty-three years of age. He was living in Salem, Massachusetts, in 1637, and was there admitted a freeman the next year. His wife's name was Mary, and their daughter Mary was baptized in Salem on the 29th of March, 1640, and their son John born on the 15th of October, 1643. The family removed to Southold as early as 1652.

The next year, the father was at New Haven
with Thomas Moore; and he was there in
1655 also, with John Budd and others. He
had business in that place, in this latter year,
about the will of James Haines, to which he
had been a witness in 1652. He is said to
have died in 1655. Letters of administration
were granted to his widow, Mary Herbert.
His estate was appraised on the 5th of September, 1658, by William Wells and Thomas
Moore, and the inventory amounted to £249
19s. His widow lived at least three years
after the death of her husband. [Moore's
" Indexes."] The Rev. John Davenport wrote
on the 4th of August, 1658, to the right wor-
shipful John Winthrop, and said, among other
things : "Mr Harbert of Southold is so ill at
Manhadoes that there is little if any hope of
his life." See Rev. Dr. Bacon's Historical
Discourses, page 373. If this was our John
Herbert of the first generation, and there
seems to have been no other of the name
known to have been here, he must have died
in 1658.

The son John owned land at Orient, " Oyster Ponds," in 1665, and gave a quit-claim to
the inhabitants of the Town for several par-

cels in 1693. In 1699, he delivered deeds for lands to Jonathan Paine and Joseph Swezey, and in 1700 he gave a deed to John Tuthill for one hundred acres in Orient. He was then living in Reading, Massachusetts. Twelve years later, he sold fifty acres on the Sound to John Paine. It was in 1699 that he made the deed for the land whereon the present church edifice, as well as the parsonage, now stands. This property and all other property which the Church was using passed, of course, into the hands of the Board of Trustees of the Church when the State of New York, soon after the close of the Revolutionary war, on the 6th of April, 1784, in the seventh session of the Legislature, held in the city of New York, enacted a law, to enable all the religious denominations in this State to appoint Trustees, to be a Body Corporate, for the purpose of taking care of the temporalities of the respective congregations, and for other purposes therein mentioned. The preamble of this law recites the thirty-eighth article of the Constitution of the State, and declares the duty of Government to encourage virtue and religion. The first article of the act makes it lawful for the male persons of full age in the congregations to elect Trustees. The second section prescribes the mode of election. The third section requires the officers of the election to file a certificate duly attested to be recorded by the Clerk of the County in a book to be kept by him for the purpose. The fourth section enacts "that the said persons so to be elected, returned, and registered shall be and hereby are declared to be the trustees for the said church, congregation or society for which they shall be so chosen, and shall be and hereby are authorized and empowered to take into their charge, care, custody and possession all the temporalities belonging to the said church, congregation or society, for which they shall be elected trustees, whether the same consist of lands, tenements, hereditaments, goods or chattels, and whether the same shall have been given, granted or devised directly to the said church, congregation or society, or to any persons in trust to and for their use; and although such gift, grant or devise may not have strictly been agreeable to the rigid rules of law, or might on strict construction be defeated by the operation of the statutes of mortmain." This fourth section also enacts that

the said trustees shall be a body corporate
and "shall lawfully have, hold, use, exercise
and enjoy all and singular the churches, meeting houses, parsonages, burying places, and
lands thereunto belonging, with the hereditaments and appurtenances heretofore by the
said church, congregation or society held, occupied or enjoyed by whatsoever name or
names, person or persons, the same were purchased and had, or to them given or granted,
or by them or any of them used and enjoyed
for the uses aforesaid, to them and their successors, to the sole and only proper use and
benefit of them the said trustees and their
successors forever, in as full, firm and ample
a manner in the law as if the said trustees
had been legally incorporated and made capable in law to take, receive, purchase, have,
hold, use and enjoy the same at and before
the purchasing, taking, receiving and holding
of the said churches, meeting houses, parsonages, burying places, and lands thereunto belonging, and lawfully had, held, and enjoyed
the same ; any law, usage, or custom to the
contrary hereof, in any wise notwithstanding."

This law, it is highly probable, was written
by the Hon. Ezra L'Hommedieu, a member

of the First Church of Southold. He was the most prominent member of the church and the most eminent citizen of the town, and perhaps of the county, at the time. He had represented the Island in the Congress of the United States as a member from the State of New York during the course of the Revolutionary war, four years from 1779 to 1783 ; and after the establishment of peace and independence, he deemed it his duty to enter the Senate of the State and take the chief place in the Legislature, in order most wisely to shape the great body of legislation which the condition of the country and the circumstances of the time demanded. He was a member of the State Senate sixteen consecutive years, from 1784 to 1799 except one year in 1792-3. He had been a member of all the Provincial Congresses of New York, including the Fourth, which framed and adopted at Kingston the First Constitution of the State, in the Spring of 1777. He was in 1801 a member of the celebrated Convention which was elected to interpret some of the parts of the Constitution of the State, and to determine how many members there should be in each house of the Legislature. He was re-

peatedly a member of the Council of Appointment which had the power until 1821 to se-
lect nearly every civil, military and judicial
officer of the Commonwealth.   He was the
foremost of all men who had lived all their
life from birth to death in Southold.   From
1787 till his death, Sebtember 28, 1811,
he was a Regent of the State University.   He
did much to give prominence to Gen. William
Floyd, whose sister was his wife.   As the
Chairman of the Judiciary Committee of the
Senate, he wrote many of the laws which were
enacted by the Legislature, after the establishment of peace, when the State of New York
began the most magnificent career of enterprise and prosperity under the operation of
these laws.   Among the most beneficent of
these wise and salutary enactments was this
statute for the election of Trustees of Churches.   According to the power and directions
of this general law, the First Church of Southold was the earliest in Suffolk County—the
earliest on Long Island also—to elect its trustees and file its certificate of incorporation.*

---

* Flatbush elected Trustees of its Reformed Dutch
Church, July 31, 1784.   Furman's, "Antiquities of Long
Island," pp, 125, 126.

20

See Book A of Certificates of Religious Cor-
porations, page 1, in the County Clerk's office for the first certificate recorded as follows,
namely :

"We, William Horton and Freegift Wells,
the Deacons of the First Church, Congregation or Society in Southold, do by these presents certify, that on Tuesday the twenty-ninth
day of June at two o'clock in the afternoon
of the same day an election was held at the
meeting house of the said first congregation
or society in Southold for the purpose of
choosing Trustees for taking the charge of
the estate and property belonging to the said
congregation agreeably to an Act of the Legislature passed the sixth of April 1784 entitled ' an Act to enable all religious Denominations in this State to appoint Trustees,' &c.
Which said meeting holding the said election
being duly notified at the said time and place,
the electors present qualified to vote by a
majority of voices did elect Deacon Freegift
Wells, Jared Landon, Esquire, and Major
Joshua Goldsmith, Trustees of the Temporalities of the first congregation or society in
Southold

"That immediately after the said election the
said Trustees were divided by Lott into three
classes, and the seat of Jared Landon, Esquire,
being the first class, becomes vacant at the
expiration of the first year ; the seat of Major

Joshua Goldsmith being the second class becomes vacant at the expiration of the second year ; and the seat of Deacon Wells being the third class becomes vacant at the expiration of the third year.

" That there being no elders or church wardens belonging to the said congregation, we the above named William Horton and Freegift Wells, Deacons as aforesaid, presided at the said election and are the returning officers thereof as directed by the said act.

WILLIAM HORTON.
FREEGIFT WELLS."

" Southold, June 29, 1784.

Suffolk County, ss.

" Personally appeared before me Thomas Youngs, Esquire, one of the Judges of the Inferior Court of Common Pleas in and for the said County, William Horton and Freegift Wells, Deacons of the First Church, Congregation or Society in Southold, and acknowledged the within certificate to be their act and deed, and I having examined the same do allow it to be recorded.

" Attest : THOMAS YOUNGS, Judge.

" Recorded the 4th of April 1785.

E. L'HOMMEDIEU, Clk."

Our worthy church-member who probably wrote the law for the appointment of Trustees, most likely wrote also the certificate of the

election of the Trustees of Southold, as well
as recorded it.   He was the Clerk of Suffolk
County for twenty-seven consecutive years
from 1784 to 1811, except the year 1810.   The
Judge who attested the certificate of the election of the trustees was also a member of the
Southold congregation.   Major Joshua Goldsmith succeeded Freegift Wells in the office
of Deacon on the death of the latter.

It is the distinctive quality of a corporation
that it never dies, and so the Board of Trustees have continued uninterruptedly for nearly
an hundred years past to hold and use according to law and justice all the property of every
kind that was in the possession and use of
the Church, or had been purchased or given
for its support or benefit, at the time when
the law of the State required them to take
the said property into their hands : and so in
due season the church edifice and parsonage
were built on the land purchased from Herbert for religious purposes.

The increase of the people, or some other
motive, caused them in 1699 to build a gallery
in the west end of the Meeting House ; and
the next year, they built one in the east end.
See Town Records, Book D, pp. 9, 113.

The bill for the latter is found in the Town Records thus in D. 5 :

" The Town of Southold Dr.
To Samuel Clarke for
building ye gallere £15 10s .
Received of Samuel Clarke for boards
and nails left of ye gallere £00–04
Paid Jacob Conklin for banesters £1–05–00
Samuel Conklin for bringing
ye banesters 0–06–09
Joshua Wells for carting
timber for ye gallere, nine shillings."

Other expenses at this period are made known by these bills, namely :

" Paid Seargeant John Corwin £5 for sweep-ing the Meeting. House the year 1790." [Town Records, Book D, p. 9.]

" 1701. Hannah Corwin, sweeping Meeting House and tending with ye Baptissm bason £2–01–08."

" 1702. The same."

The year 1701 was marked by a transac-tion whose causes are not distinctly indicated. This was the Pastor's sale of his home to the people—the same home which they had con-veyed to him on condition of his settlement as their pastor twenty-seven years previously. Why he wished to sell, or they wished to pur-chase, at this time, can only be inferred from

the known facts in the case. He did not begin his ministry until he was forty-five years
old, and had nearly reached the period of life
in which many congregations at the present
day are inclined to deem a minister too aged
to continue in the pastoral work. He had
been the pastor nearly twenty-seven years in
1701, and had two years previously reached
his three score and ten years. It was not to
be expected that he would be able to cultivate
his farm and also perform his ministerial duties without embarrassment for a much longer
period. It evidently seemed desirable to the
people that he should be relieved from the
care and labor and business of his farm, and
continue his pastoral activity in his extreme
old age free from this burden. They seem to
have always most thoroughly considered his
wants, esteemed his ministerial character, and
appreciated his pastoral services. Though
he had passed beyond the Psalmist's line of
three score years and ten, they sustained him
in his old age with all the more tenderness,
and with the reverence due to the hoary head
that is in the way of righteousness. They accordingly bought his dwelling and the farm
on which it stood, and determined that it

should be perpetually the parsonage for himself and his successors, and so it proved to be for nearly an hundred years. They raised the money to pay for it in the same way that they assessed and collected taxes for other public uses.

The next year, they gave it the repairs which more than a quarter of a century's duration and use had caused it to need.

For some years from this date, it was necessary for the people of Southold to act with caution. A new Governor reached New York in May, 1702. This was Edward Hyde, Lord Cornbury, eldest son of the Earl of Clarendon. He was a reckless adventurer, without principle or virtue, who had fled from his native country to avoid his creditors. He was eager to gain wealth from his office, and cared nothing for justice. He received many instructions from his cousin, Queen Anne ; but he was careful to follow those only that suited his own inclinations. He was directed among other things to tolerate all forms of religion, but to do his utmost to make the Church of England the Established Church of his Provinces. In the Province of New York previous to 1699 the Church of England had but one minister except the chaplains of the military forces, and in the Province of New Jersey not one. Trinity Church in New York city was built in 1696-7, under the Governorship of Benjamin Fletcher, who arrived in New York in 1692, and who had two chief objects in view, namely: the promotion of his own personal interests and especially the increase of his wealth, and secondly, the introduction of the English Church into the Province. In 1693 he induced the Assembly to pass an act providing for the building of a church in the city of New York, another in Richmond, two in Westchester, and two in Suffolk, and the settlement of a Protestant minister in each of those churches with a salary that might range from forty to an hundred pounds—the whole expense to be paid by a tax laid on all the inhabitants. Provision was also made for the division of all the province into parishes. The Governor restricted the word Protestant and wrested it to mean Episcopal, and under this act the building of Trinity Church was begun in 1696 and was opened for public worship February 6, 1697. The minister was the Rev. William Vesey, who had been an Independent minister in Queens county, and who never had a very desirable reputation ; but he succeeded in 1703 in obtaining for this church a gift of the King's farm, which laid the foundation of the millions of wealth now belonging to Trinity church. He complained in 1699 of the discomforts of his new situation. He did not find the favor with the Governors Bellamont and Hunter that he desired, and the former described him "as capable of any wickedness, base, unchristian ; his wickedness is plain ; he wants honesty." He was not the only Episcopal minister in the Province when Lord Cornbury became Governor in 1702. There were also two others, Messrs Stuart and Barton. It was with these three Episcopal ministers only in the Province that the Governor determined and attempted to establish the Episcopal Church as the State Church. Soon after he came from England a terrible disease (probably yellow fever) was brought to New York from St. Thomas, West Indies. It spread rapidly, and proved fatal in nearly every case. The inhabitants of the city fled in every direction, and especially to Long Island. The Governor and his Council sought to escape the pestilence by fleeing to Jamaica. This was a prosperous village of

Presbyterians. They had recently built a
beautiful Church and had bought a house and
glebe for their minister. There were more
than one hundred families of them, " exem-
plary for all Christian knowledge and good-
ness." Their Church was worth six hundred
pounds, and the manse and glebe twice as
valuable. Indeed, the manse was the best
house in the village. The minister was the
Rev. John Hubbard, a native of Ipswich,
Massachusetts, who graduated at Harvard in
1695. When he heard of the Governor's
coming, he removed to a smaller dwelling,
and offered the use of the parsonage to Lord
Cornbury, who accepted the hospitality and
repaid it in a very peculiar way, namely : by
turning the pastor and his flock out of the
Church and handing it over to an Episcopal
minister named Barton. Nor was this all.
For when the Governor returned to New
York, he put the Episcopal minister into possession of the parsonage also, which was occupied, thenceforth, as his residence ; and the
Presbyterians had to carry on a law-suit for
twenty years before they recovered the possession and use of their Church. Cornbury
also ordered the Sheriff unlawfully to take the

parsonage-land away from Mr. Hubbard; to divide it into lots; and to lease it for the benefit of the Episcopalians. This was done, and its owners deemed it too dangerous even to ask for the redress of their wrongs. This was the same Lord Cornbury who imprisoned for two months the Rev. Messrs. Hampton and Makemie, two Presbyterian ministers, for preaching in New York city and in Newtown. After living for years in the most shameless profligacy, he was at length deprived of his governorship by his kinswoman, Queen Anne. His creditors immediately seized him and kept him in prison in the City Hall on Wall Street, until the death of his father raised him from his cell to the peerage of Great Britain, and gave him a seat in the House of Lords.

During this Governor's administration, the Rev. Mr. Hobart and his puritan people in Southold had to walk softly; and we find nothing here to chronicle in those years.

On the arrival of Governor Hunter, a Scotchman, affairs assumed a different aspect in New York city, and throughout the province. The people of Southold seem to have improved it to build a new meeting house; but the new structure, however satisfactory in

most respects, did not please the people in
the pitch of its roof. Hence they voted, in
1711, to take it down and build "a flatter
roof upon the Meeting House;" and in the
following year, order was taken to seat the
people in this house according to rank, dignity, official duties, and other considerations.
[Town Records, Book D, page 117.]

For more than three score and ten years
now the people of the town had been spread-
ing abroad, and especially eastward and westward, from the meeting house. Some of
them were more than ten miles away from it
in one direction, and others were equally distant in the opposite quarter. The minister
was midway between eighty and ninety years
of age. The people were increasing in number and in wealth, as well as in the occupation
of the soil in the parts of the town remote
from the centre. Both in the east and the
west, there began to be indications of a desire for public worship at points nearer than
the site of the original settlement. The supply of ministers was also increasing. In the
creation of this supply, Yale was now effectively supplementing the good work of Harvard. In 1702, the only graduate of the Con-

necticut College became a minister. The case was the same in 1703. Ten of the twelve graduates of the next three years became ministers, including Jonathan Dickinson, the first President of the College of New Jersey, while the class of 1709 yielded five clergymen, including Benjamin Woolsey, who eleven years later became the third pastor of Southold; and all the graduates of the years 1713, 1715, 1716, and 1717 became ministers. The class of 1715 included Nathaniel Mather, who was afterwards settled at Aquebogue, within the limits of this town, and the class of 1717, Joseph Lamb, who became the pastor of Mattituck, which is also in the Town of Southold.

In these circumstances, it is not surprising that James Reeve, about the year 1715, gave half an acre at Mattituck for the site of a meeting house, and one acre and a half adjoining for a burying ground; and here the Rev. Joseph Lamb was ordained the minister soon after his graduation from Yale College in 1717.

On the first day of January 1718—not in 1700, as Griffin says—David Youngs gave a deed for the site of a meeting house at Orient,

21

"Oyster Ponds," on which an edifice was
erected in that and the following years.
[Town Records, Book C, p. 67. Gardner's
Historical Sketch of the Church, page 21.]

It was in the midst of these changes that
the Rev. Joshua Hobart closed his long life
and ministry on the last day of the winter,
February 28, 1717.

Ten years later, the Town voted that a
tomb-stone be purchased to mark his grave
and honor his name. In the pecuniary accounts of the Town, with the date of October
31, 1732, appears the bill against the Town
for " the Building Mr. Hobart's tomb with
stone lime & tendence 16s 11d." [Town Records, Book " Righteous & Holy."]

The lime commonly used here, in that day,
was obtained by burning the shells of oysters,
scallops and other sea-fish; and a character-
istic specimen of the mortar made with it may
now be seen beneath the tomb-stone of Col.
John Youngs, the eldest and most eminent
son of the first pastor and the friend and contemporary of Mr. Hobart.

These tomb-stones are heavy horizontal
slabs of sandstone. The inscription on Col.
Youngs's is still legible. That of the second

pastor's was on a tablet which was set into the upper surface of the stone. The tradition is, that this tablet was destroyed by the British during the war of Independence. There are two branches of the tradition—one, that the inscription was cut upon a tablet of lead, which the British troops took for military uses; the other, that the material was marble, which was ruthlessly broken and destroyed by them. The former seems the more probable; for there are, in the oldest part of the grave yard, several other tomb-stones from which the inscription-tablets are gone.

After full twenty years of diligent search for a copy of the inscription on Mr. Hobart's tomb-stone, I was providentially able to obtain one which is well attested. It is partly in prose, and partly poetic. The latter part was written by MATHER BYLES, A. M., and it may be proper to say a word here in respect to the author.

He was born in Boston, March 26, 1706, of good parentage, his mother being a descendant of John Cotton and Richard Mather. He was graduated at Harvard College in 1725, two years before Southold ordered the tomb-stone for Mr. Hobart and seven years before

the Town paid for building the tomb.   He
became the first pastor of the Hollis Street
Church, in Boston, when he was ordained
Dec. 20, 1733.   The College of Aberdeen,
Scotland, made him D.D. in 1765.   Early in
his ministry, he became widely known as a
poet, a wit and a preacher.   Alexander Pope,
Lord Lansdown and Rev. Dr. Isaac Watts
were among his correspondents in England.
    The inscription was this:

"THE REV. JOSHUA HOBART,
BORN AT HINGHAM JULY 1629,
EXPIRED IN SOUTHOLD FEB. 28th 1716.

He was a faithful minister, a skillful physician, a general scholar, a courageous patriot, and to crown all an
eminent Christian.

Beneath the sacred honors of this tomb,
In pensive silence and majestic gloom,
The man of God conceals his reverend head
Amidst the awful mansions of the dead.
No more the statesman shall assert the laws
And in the Senate plead his country's cause :
In the sad Church no more the listening throng
Gaze on his eyes and dwell upon his tongue :
No more his healing hand shall health restore,
Elude the grave and baffle death no more.
In Eden's flowery vales his spirit roves
Where streams of life roll through the immortal groves.
Fixed in deep slumbers here the dust is given
Till the last trumpet shakes the frame of heaven.
Then new to life the waking saint shall rise,

And gay in glory, glitter up the skies.
With smiling joys and heavenly raptures crowned,
Bid endless ages wheel their never ceasing round."

His wife's grave is beside his own, and covered with a monument in every respect sim-
ilar, except that the inscription is cut into the
stone itself.   She died nineteen years earlier
than his own death, the date of her decease
being April 19, 1698, and her age fifty-six
years.

It has not been possible to trace their descendants.   Irene married Daniel Way of
Southold, but this family name here has long
since disappeared.

PART III.

PERIOD OF THE MINISTRY OF THE REV. BENJAMIN WOOLSEY.

1720–1736.

CHAPTER VI.

The third Pastor was the Rev. Benjamin
Woolsey. Here again may be seen the inti-.
mate relation between this old Church and
Town on the one hand and Yarmouth and its
neighborhood in England on the other; for
the grandfather of our third Pastor was
George Woolsey, born in Yarmouth, October
27, 1610. The place of his birth is the most
eastern borough of England. The peninsula
on which Great Yarmouth is built is remarkable for its peculiar geological formation; for
it is the bed of a former estuary. The place
is also note-worthy for its antiquities, its
quay, and its fisheries. Its Church of Saint
Nicholas [Santa Claus] was founded eight
hundred years ago. Its quay extends for a
mile north and south on the east or left bank
of the Yare, and parallel to the shore of the

sea, so that the streets of Great Yarmouth
which run east and west stretch across the
peninsula from the broad waters of the Yare
on the west to the far broader waters of the
North Sea on the east.

George Woolsey was a son of the Rev.
Benjamin Woolsey and a grandson of Thomas
Woolsey of Yarmouth.   It appears from the
investigations of Charles B. Moore, Esq., that
he had resided with his parents in the city of
Rotterdam, in Holland, and that his father
was for a time a minister in that city, where
he had been preceded by another clergyman,
previously of Yarmouth, the Rev. Dr. William
Ames.   This celebrated minister was born in
Norfolk county, England, in 1576.   He was
educated in Christ's College at the University
of Cambridge.   His religious principles and
life made him the object of persecution and
compelled him to leave the University.   He
left his native country also, and removed to
the Hague, the capital of Holland.   He became the Professor of Theology in the University of Franeker in Friesland, and performed the duties of his office satisfactorily for
twelve years.   He then removed to Rotterdam, and became a pastor in that great com-

mercial city, where he had very many English
hearers, and lived until his death in 1633.
The Rev. Hugh Peters, afterwards of Salem,
Massachusetts, and the Rev. Thomas Hooker,
the founder of Hartford, Connecticut, were
some time his assistant ministers. He was
an able and spirited controversial writer
against Cardinal Bellarmine and others. His
Medulla Theologiæ was famous in its day.
He was a member of the celebrated Synod of
Dordrecht, which held its memorable sessions
in the year 1618-9, and defined the faith of
the Reformed Dutch Church on the five
points of election, redemption, depravity, ir-
resistible grace, and perseverence in the
Christian life. In this Synod there were representatives of the English church and of other
Reformed communions, and it settled the doctrine and order of the Church in the Netherlands as well as in the numerous and popu-
lous colonies thereof.

After the death of the Rev. Dr. Ames, his
widow with his daughter and his two sons returned to Yarmouth, whence they sailed in
May, 1637, on board the Mary Anne, for Salem in New England. Mr. Moore holds that
this vessel probably brought over at that time

the family of the Rev. John Youngs, our first
Pastor, and that it was with reference to the
voyage of the Mary Anne that the Commissioners of Emigration examined the Rev.
John Youngs, his wife Joan, and their six
children and forbade his passage.

It is very likely that the Rev. Mr. Youngs
himself crossed over the North Sea to Holland and from that country came to America.

It is believed that George Woolsey came
over in a Dutch vessel with Dutch emigrants
in 1623, during his thirteenth year, and went
to Plymouth in New England. It is to be
remembered, that the pilot or navigator of
the Mayflower was a Hollander, or Dutchman,
and that the Mayflower company desired and
intended, when they left the harbor at the
mouth of the Ply in England, to make their
home in America near their Dutch friends on
Manhattan Island. Most of them had been
intimate with the Dutch in Holland, and were
grateful for the protection and freedom which
had been granted to them in that country.

George Woolsey became a resident of the
Dutch metropolis at the mouth of the Hud-
son, and a trader in partnership with Isaac
Allerton, who had come to Plymouth in the

Mayflower three years earlier than himself. He was a witness before the Governor and Council on the 23d of July, 1647, and gave his testimony on a charge affecting the character and official conduct of the chief financial officer of the colony. On the 10th of August, 1647, he bought of Thomas Robertson a house and plantation in Flushing, L. I. On the 9th of December, in the same year, he was married at the Dutch Church in New York to Rebekah Cornell, a sister of Sarah Cornell, whose first husband was Thomas Willett, formerly of Bristol, England, and whose second husband was Charles Bridges, of New York city. George and Rebekah (Cornell) Woolsey had a daughter Sarah, who was baptized at the Reformed Dutch Church, New York, August 7, 1650. Their son George, born October 10, 1652, received baptism three days later, one of the sponsors being Elsje, i. e., Alice Newton, wife of Governor Stuyvesant's celebrated military officer, Captain Bryan Newton, who became one of the patentees of the Town of Jamaica, Long Island, where George Woolsey, Jr., became a prominent citizen, and where in 1680 he made an arrangement with Captain and Mrs. New-

22

ton to care for them in their old age and to own their land after their death.   See Charles B. Moore's Bryan Newton in New York, G. and B. Record, July, 1876.

In 1648, George Woolsey and three others were appointed fire-wardens of the city of New York, with large powers of inspection and control.   See Booth's New York, p. 133. He became the owner of land at Jamaica by deed from the Town, February 15, 1664.   He was one of the Patentees, and, as one of its first settlers, this was probably the place of his residence for more than thirty years.   He was chosen Town Clerk in 1673, and his hand writing is plainly legible in the Town Records. He made his will on the 2nd of November, 1691, and died August 17, 1698, being nearly eighty-eight years of age.   The proof of his will was made on the 22d of February, 1699, and the record of it is in the Queens County Records, Vol. A, p. 132.   He bequeathed to his eldest son, George, his land at Beaver Pond, to his son Thomas fifteen acres on the west of the home-lot of Anton Waters, to his son John thirty acres by the Little Plains, an out-fit to his daughter Mary on her marriage or when she attains the age of eighteen years, and the rest of his estate to his wife Rebekah. At her decease, the lands and tenements in her use to be equally divided to his three sons, and the goods and chattels to his three daughters Sarah (Hallett), Rebekah (Wiggins), and Mary Woolsey. When he died, his grandson Benjamin Woolsey, our third Pastor, was in his eleventh year.

His son George Woolsey, Jr., became a prominent citizen of Jamaica. He was made Captain in 1696. His wife's name was Hannah. They had two sons—George and Benjamin—named after their paternal ancestors.

George Woolsey, the elder of these sons, was born in New York, October 10, 1682, and removed in his early manhood, between 1700 and 1710, from Jamaica to Pennington, New Jersey, where he bought two hundred and eighteen acres of good land, which he made his homestead. He died before March 11, 1762, when his will was proved. See the Rev. Dr. George Hale's History of the First Presbyterian Church of Pennington. His descendants have been eminent generally for their religious character and moral worth. His homestead has never ceased to be the home of his male descendants, and is now

(1876) the homestead of his great-grand-son, George Woolsey, a Deacon of the First Presbyterian Church of Pennington, who was for three years a senator of the State of New Jersey, and whose son, Theodore Frelinghuysen Woolsey, with his wife and six children, lives on the homestead with his aged father.

Benjamin, the second son of Captain George Woolsey, Jr., and his wife Hannah, was born at Jamaica, November 19, 1687. They sold to this son in 1722, while he was our third Pastor, the land at Beaver Pond, Jamaica, on which they were then living, for three hundred pounds sterling.

After the removal of our pastor to Dosoris in 1736, his aged father lived with him, and died there, January 19, 1740-1, where his tomb is to be found to this day.

The Rev. Benjamin Woolsey was graduated at Yale College in the class of 1709, midway between the origin of the College and its removal from Saybrook to New Haven. His class numbered nine graduates, and in respect to social standing, which was the principle of arrangement in the Catalogue at that time, he held the central place in the class. Yale had graduated seven classes previous to the graduation of Mr. Woolsey's; and according to the latest General Catalogue of the College, these seven classes numbered altogether twenty-two graduates; of whom eighteen became ministers. The first sixteen classes of Yale numbered sixty-one graduates, and all of them became ministers except fourteen. The graduates of this College in those years became ministers in nearly as large a proportion as the graduates of the best Theological Seminaries do now.

This shows the character of Mr. Woolsey's fellow students and associates in College. He had attained his twenty-second year when he was graduated, and five years later he was married to Abigail Taylor, a daughter of John Taylor of Oyster Bay, Long Island, and of Mary (Whitehead) Taylor. John Taylor died in 1735, and left to Mrs. Woolsey a valuable estate of several hundred acres near Glen Cove.

Soon after his graduation at Yale College, Mr. Woolsey began the work of the ministry and preached in several places. One instance of his preaching became famous. This occurred while he was visiting his elder brother,

George, in Hopewell, now Pennington, New Jersey, where, as we have seen, the Woolseys were, as they have been from the beginning and are now, among the most worthy, pious, and influential people. He preached in the Episcopal church in Hopewell, and his being allowed to do this was one of the charges of wrong doing brought in 1712 against Governor Hunter by the Rev. Jacob Henderson, an Irishman, who had been sent to this country in 1710 by the Church of England Society for the propagation of the Gospel in Foreign Parts. The controversy between Governor Hunter and the Episcopal ministers who supported his administration in religious affairs on the one side, and on the other side the ministers of the same denomination who opposed his proceedings, was sharp and bitter, each flatly contradicting the other's statements. See Documentary History of New York; documents pertaining to the Colonial History of this State; Webster's History of the Presbyterian Church, page 353; Sprague's Annals of the American Pulpit, Vol. 5, p. 34. But whatever the consequences of his ministry to himself or to others, Mr. Woolsey did not cease to preach the gospel. On the con-

trary, he proclaimed the divine word whenever he was providentially called to utter it
as the minister of Jesus Christ. In this way
it came to pass that he was installed the Pastor of the First Church of Southold in July,
1720.

Autograph of the Rev. Benjamin Woolsey in 1721.

Here he fulfilled the duties of his office for
sixteen years. He had the satisfaction of seeing the intellectual and spiritual life of the
Church and Town flourish under his ministry.

Among the fruits of this life was the pro-
duction of several pious and aspiring young
men who were an honor to their native place
and a benefit to other parts of the country in
which they lived during their later years.

Abner Reeve, a son of Thomas Reeve, was
born in Southold in 1710. He acquired a
liberal education. Having finished the course
of studies in Yale College, he was graduated
in the class of 1731, when he was twenty-one
years of age. He studied theology three or
four years, and was licensed in Southold to

preach the gospel, in 1735. He settled in
the same year at Nesaquake in Smithtown.
He was the first minister who ever resided in
that town.   His disposition was amiable and
his scholarship excellent; but his habits were
somewhat eccentric, and the social customs of
the times led him into the intemperate use of
strong drink, so that he was for a time laid
aside from the ministry, after he had served
as a licensed preacher at Smithtown, Fire
Place, and Huntington for ten or twelve years.
He returned to his native place in Southold,
and here, under the faithful ministry of our
fifth pastor, the Rev. William Throop, he was
restored to sobriety and the life of godliness.

The people of Moriches and Ketchabonnach
obtained his services, and on the sixth of November, 1755, the Presbytery of Suffolk, in
"the Western Meeting House," organized
the church of Moriches and ordained and installed him as its Pastor.   At his request, the
Rev. William Throop, of Southold, was invited
to preach the sermon; and accordingly Mr.
Throop preached from this text, I. Cor 9 : 27.
" But I keep under my body, and bring it into
subjection: lest that by any means when I

have preached to others, I myself should be a castaway."

Mr. Reeve was the Pastor of Moriches for eight years. Having been dismissed in 1763, he settled in Blooming Grove, Orange County, New York. He withdrew from the Presbytery of New York in 1770, and afterwards became the minister of Burlington, Vermont, where he remained until his death, in 1795, at the age of eighty-five years.

The Rev. Ezra Reeve was the eldest son of the Rev. Abner Reeve, and was born in 1733, and honors the Town of Southold, the place of his birth. He prepared for College in his boyhood and having finished the regular course he was graduated at Yale in 1757, being in the same class with the eminent Judge and United States Senator John Sloss Hobart and the famous Gov. Edmund Fanning, who was a Southold man. Mr. Reeve was ordained and installed the first Pastor of Holland, Hampden county, Massachusetts, September 13, 1765, the year that the Church was organized. He fulfilled his ministry faithfully, and died there April 25, 1818, aged eighty-five years.

The Rev. Abner Reeve's wife was Mary

Topping; and one of their sons was named
after her family; but in his case, *Tapping* has
become the established *spelling*. It was
while his parents lived at Fire Place, in the
Town of Brook Haven, that Tapping Reeve
was born in October 1744. He prepared for
College, studied in Princeton, and was graduated in 1763, the same year that his father
was released from the pastoral care of Moriches. While he was in Princeton, he formed an acquanitance with the only daughter of
the President of the College, the Rev. Aaron
Burr, and in due season, he married her.
She was a grand-daughter of Jonathan Edwards, the father-in-law and successor of Mr.
Burr as President of the College of New Jersey, and her only brother was the third Vice
President of the United States.

Tapping Reeve settled in Litchfield, Connecticut; founded the celebrated Law School
of that place; and became the Chief Justice
of the State. He was the head of the School
for nearly forty years, and taught a larger
number of the most eminent lawyers in the
United States than any man of his own generation or of any previous age. On his death,
Dec. 13, 1823, his pastor, the Rev. Dr. Ly-

man Beecher, said of him: "I have never known a man who loved so many persons and was himself beloved by so many." He was the first lawyer of prominence in this country who labored to make a change in the laws controlling the property of married women.

Another of the boys who grew up under Mr. Woolsey's ministry was Simon Horton. His parents were Joshua Horton, Ensign, and Eliza or Elizabeth (Grover) Horton. His mother was a daughter of Simon Grover, whose wife was Elizabeth, daughter of Thomas Moore. Joshua Horton, Ensign, was a son of Joshua Horton son of the original Barnabas.

Simon Horton was born March 30, 1711. According to the tradition of the family, both himself and his second cousin, the Rev. Azariah Horton, were born in the dwelling of their great-grandfather, the old Barnabas Horton house, which is still (1876) occupied, though more than two hundred and thirty years old.* He was graduated at Yale in the

*Torn down in October and November, 1878. The new one on the old site is now (1878) owned and occupied by Mr. David P. Horton.

same class with his townsman, Abner Reeve,
in 1731. He pursued his theological studies,
most likely with his pastor, for a few years,
and some time between September, 1734, and
September, 1735, he was ordained by the
Presbytery of East Jersey, and installed as
the first pastor of Connecticut Farms, four or
five miles from the city of Elizabeth, New
Jersey. His parish covered a large extent of
territory, and included the present parish of
Springfield, New Jersey. He belonged to
the New Side in the Presbyterian church, as
might be inferred from his associations. He
removed from Connecticut Farms in 1746,
and was succeeded there by Southold's fourth
pastor, the Rev. James Davenport, while he
himself was installed as the successor of the
Rev. Samuel Pomeroy in the pastoral office
at Newtown, Long Island.

Here he fulfilled the duties of his office
until 1772, when he resigned, and thereafter
resided with his son-in-law, Judge Benjamin
Coe, of Newtown. During the later years of
his life, he was sent by the Presbytery yearly
to supply the East and West Houses on Stat-
en Island. He died May, 8, 1786. He was
twice married—first to Abigail Howell, who

died May 5, 1752, and secondly, January 7, 1762, to Elizabeth Fish. His only child was Phœbe, who became the wife of Judge Coe. Throughout the War of Independence, he was an earnest and active patriot, and was driven with his son-in-law from his home by the British. They found a refuge in Warwick, Orange County, New York.

The Newtown congregation was so thoroughly scattered by the war, that only five of its communicants remained at the return of peace. The British and Tories had utterly ruined the Church building.

The Rev. Simon Horton was a man of medium size, good character, devoted piety, and solemn deportment.

His successor at Newtown in the pastoral office was the Rev. Nathan Woodhull, a native of Brook Haven, Long Island.

A few years younger than Simon Horton, and born in the same old Barnabas Horton house, was Azariah Horton, a son of Jonathan, whose father was Jonathan, the youngest son and principal heir of Barnabas, succeeding him in the possession of the homestead. Azariah's mother, the wife of Jonathan Horton, Jr., was Mary Tuthill. Her family was one of the earliest in the Town, John Tuthill being the chief executive officer thereof in 1642 by appointment or recognition of the General Court for the Jurisdiction of the New Haven Colony, including the Town of Southold; and the members of the Tuthill family, descendants of Henry Tuthill, are now more numerous, and together possess more taxable property, than those of any other family in the Town.

Azariah Horton was born March 20, 1715. His boyhood was bright and virtuous; and having prepared for College, he entered Yale, and pursued the full course of studies. He was graduated in the class of 1735, being ranked in social standing second below President Burr and sixth above the Rev. Dr. Bellamy. He prepared himself after his graduation more particularly for the ministry, and was ordained by the Presbytery of New York in 1740. He received a call to settle in a desirable parish on Long Island; but he declined this call, in order to labor for the more destitute heathen, especially the Shinnecocks in the Town of Southampton; and for nine years, from 1741 to 1750, he was a missionary among the Indians of Long Island.

REV. AZARIAH HORTON. 267

There was in Edinburgh, Scotland, a "Society for Propagating Christian Knowledge;" and it was this Society that supported the Missionaries David and John Brainerd, as well as Azariah Horton, in their labors for the Indians. Here is an extract from Minutes of this Society:

"Edinburgh, 2d November, 1749. "The Correspondents at New York had likewise sent hither journals of the Rev'd Mr. John Brainerd, from the 1st May, 1748, to 7th September, 1749, and of Azariah Horton from the 26th August, 1748, to the 9th April, 1749, as Missionary Ministers employed by this Society for the conversion of the infidel Indian natives living upon the borders of the Provinces of New York, New Jersey, and Pennsylvania, bearing their diligence and success in their mission." See Rev. Dr. Thomas Brainerd's Life of the Rev. John Brainerd, pp. 157, 158.

Some of Azariah Horton's Journals, thus kept for the Scotch Missionary Society that employed him, were printed, and quotations from them are found in Prime's History of Long Island and in Furman's Antiquities of Long Island.

He went in 1742 to the Forks of the Delaware (Delaware and Lehigh rivers at Easton,

Pa.), to prepare the Indians there for the ministry of Brainerd. Like his cousin Simon Horton, he was a New Side man in his sympathies and associations.

In a letter written at Southampton, September 14, 1751, he speaks of the annoyance which " The Separates " were causing him, and the same spirit causes annoyance in these days to the faithful, intelligent and worthy ministration of the gospel for the spiritual welfare of the Shinnecock tribe.

When his work among the Indians, as a missionary to the heathen, became essentially accomplished, he withdrew from the field, and became the first Pastor of the Church of Madison, New Jersey, in 1751, this church having been formed by taking a part of Hanover for the purpose in 1748. He faithfully served this church for twenty-five years, and then resigned his charge in November, 1776. On the 27th of March in the next year, he died. The inscription on his tomb-stone in the old church yard is this :

" In memory of the Rev. Azariah Horton, for 25 years Pastor of this Church. Died March 27, 1777, aged 62 years."

The volume of Barber and Howe's Historical Collections of New Jersey, page 377, gives this inscription. Some twenty years since, an unknown gentleman appeared in Madison and set up a more beautiful monument at the Rev. Azariah Horton's grave. Mr. Horton's only son died in Philadelphia.

The Rev. Theodore L. Cuyler, D. D., is one of the descendants of the Rev. Azariah Horton. See Horton Genealogy by George F. Horton, M.D., Philadelphia, 1876, p. 184.

Thomas Youngs, another of the lads under Mr. Woolsey's ministry, was born here in 1719. Having prepared for College and pursued the course of studies in Yale, he was graduated in the class of 1741, a class eminent for the ability of its members, containing Governor Livingston of New Jersey, Rev. Drs. Mansfield, Hopkins, Buell, Sproat, and Welles, with Rev. Messrs. Stephen Williams, David Brainerd, Thomas Lewis, David Youngs, and other distinguished men.

Thomas Youngs became the Judge of his native County, and a member of the State Legislature, in which he served his country from 1784 to 1786. His death occurred on the 19th of February, 1793. He was a son of Judge Joshua Youngs, who was a son of

Zerubbabel, whose father was Col. John
Youngs, the eldest son of the first Pastor.

Thomas Youngs married Rhoda Budd, and
made his home in that part of the Town
which was then called Stirling, and near the
present Stirling Creek.   He owned about his
house some five hundred acres of land, east
of Greenport, and extending from Long Isl-
and Sound to Gardiner's Bay.   He held his
land firmly, and his son Thomas, who became
its possessor after the death of the Judge, followed his example.   It is now the property of
the Judge's grand-sons and their heirs, and
of the Hon. David G. Floyd, and the heirs of
the Hon. Frederick W. Lord, A.M., M.D.

David Youngs, a kinsman of Judge Thomas
Youngs, and born in the same Town and in
the same year, 1719, was a fellow student in
the same class and received his degree from
Yale at the same time.   The Rev. Dr. Samuel Hopkins, of Newport, Rhode Island, his
College class-mate, commended him as excel-
ling Brainerd and Buell in fervency of spirit
and Christian zeal.   He became the Pastor of
Brook Haven. This Congregation, on the
29th of May, 1742, besought the Presbytery
of New Brunswick to ordain him, and the

Presbytery granted the request, and ordained him on the 12th of October, 1742. In 1746, the year after the formation of the Synod of New York, the Presbytery of New Brunswick gave him leave to join the Presbytery of New York on account of its being more convenient to him to be a member of the latter body. In May, 1749, he became a member of the Presbytery of Suffolk by vote and direction of the Synod of New York. He died before May 27, 1752 ; for on this day the Presbytery of Suffolk made a record of his death as follows :

" Since our last session, [September 18, 1751], the Rev. Mr. David Youngs of Brook Haven departed this life." See Suffolk Presbytery's Records. p. 20.

" The Separates " had greatly weakened his congregation, and the consequences are visible within the bounds of the Setauket parish until this day.

Migration from Southold westward has never ceased from the earliest years of our history till the present time. Every State of the Union most likely contains families or individuals whose ancestors went forth from this swarming hive. The more westward

Towns of Long Island; Orange County, New York; Elizabeth, New Jersey, and the region about it; and several places in Morris County, New Jersey, received many inhabitants from this place during the first century of its history. The Town of Chester, Morris County, New Jersey, for example, may be regarded as a colony from the East End of Long Island. The founders of the Presbyterian Church were mainly from the Hamptons. The Congregational Church shows a preponderance of Southold names. The Town of Chester was territorially formed from Roxbury in 1799. Barber and Howe say:

"The first permanent settlement in the Township was made by emigrants from Long Island, who founded the Presbyterian Church." See Historical Collections, page 379.

The Rev. Frank A. Johnson, Pastor of the Congregational Church of Chester, in a Centennial Historical Discourse, on the 2d of July, 1876, makes this quotation:

"The tract of land now constituting the Township of Chester was surveyed and run into lots in 1713 and 1714, and began soon after to be settled with emigrants from Southold, Long Island."

He adds:

" It was in their hearts to do as their fathers had done: plant a church of the same faith and form of government as that in which they had been baptized and to which they owed so much."

The Pastor of the Presbyterian Church of Chester, New Jersey, as well as the Congregational Pastor, has kindly given me information in respect to that Town and its settlement.

The Presbyterian Pastor is the Rev. James F. Brewster, a descendant of the Rev. Nathaniel Brewster, the first Pastor of Brook Haven, Long Island, who was a grandson of William Brewster, the Ruling Elder of the Pilgrims who came to Plymouth in the Mayflower.

In the Historical Sermon which the Rev. James F. Brewster preached in the Presbyterian Church of Chester, July 2, 1876, he said :

" More than a century and a quarter ago a little band of Presbyterian pioneers from the eastern end of Long Island—a section which has ever been a stronghold of Presbyterianism —brought among these hills the faith and worship of their fathers, and, like the ancient patriarch, they built their altar and called upon their God, on the spot which they had made their home, as soon as they were strong enough to unite themselves." "The founders of the church, with their children and their children's children, are sleeping in the dust, but their work, by God's blessing, still stands; the glorious gospel still is proclaimed, through which, as we trust, hundreds upon hundreds have here obtained salvation, and from among these hills have ascended to Heaven."

The church of Chester seems to have been divided about 1745, and a part of it to have accepted the sentiments of "the Separates," and to have maintained fellowship with this division of the Congregationalists on Long Island. The part that continued to cherish and maintain the views and principles of the churches of the standing order in New England and on Long Island, became Presbyterians; and having called a pastor, the Presbytery of New Brunswick ordained and installed him in the autumn of 1752.

There was an effort made, during the latter years of the Revolutionary war, to reunite the two churches. The effort continued indeed for six years, and throughout this period both churches had the same minister. But the attempt was not permanently successful.

About 1785, the separatical church was dissolved; but the members of it for the most part formed themselves not long afterwards into the present Congregational Church of Chester, which is deemed the oldest Congregational Church in New Jersey, and dates its organization 1747. It may be regarded as the legitimate successor of the Separatical Congregation, and the Presbyterian Church as the outgrowth of the Congregation that retained the fellowship of the New England churches of " the Standing Order."

The first pastor of the Congregational Church was the Rev. Samuel Swezey, who continued to fulfil the duties of the office for twenty years until the Revolutionary war was about to sweep the country with its storms.

The church edifice during the war became an hospital for sick and wounded soldiers of the National Army under Washington, whose headquarters were ten or twelve miles distant; and public worship in it was discontinued throughout the years 1777 and 1778. In consequence of the deprivation of Christian instruction and restraint, the moral and religious habits of the people were greatly impaired.

The Rev. James Youngs was ordained and

installed as the pastor of the new Congregational Church. He bore an early Southold
family name, like his predecessor, the Rev.
Samuel Swezey. His ministry continued until his death in November, 1790, at the early
age of thirty-two years. His death was
greatly lamented.

The church, for more than ten years thereafter, had only such irregular supplies as it
was able on occasion to obtain from Long
Island.

But on the 16th of June, 1801, the Rev.
Stephen Overton was ordained and installed
as the Pastor. He was by birth or ancestry
a Southolder. Under his ministry a new
house of worship was built in 1803, the same
year that the First Church of Southold erected
its present church building. The new edifice
of Chester was forty by fifty feet in size, with
front and side galleries, steeple and bell,
somewhat smaller than the present Southold
church edifice.

Mr. Overton's ministry continued for twenty-seven years, and only two years and a half
after his release from the pastorate, he died,
on the 18th of September, 1830.

Within the last fifty years, this church of

Chester has had several pastors and supplies. The Rev. James S. Evans, D.D., formerly pastor of Middletown, Long Island, and subsequently of Setauket, Long Island, and more recently the Long Island Synod's Superintendent of Home Missions was the pastor from 1867 to 1871, and while he labored with them in the gospel, the congregation built a parsonage.

But the old Church and Town of Southold under Mr. Woolsey's ministry were not only planting their colonies abroad ; they were also forming new centres of growth and new congregations of worshippers at home.

It was in the early part of 1718 that David Youngs gave a lot of land at Oysterponds (now Orient), for the purpose of having at some future time a Meeting House erected upon it. See Town Records, Book C, p 67. In 1725 the Meeting House was built, and it continued to be a place of public worship till 1818. But there was no regular organized church in that part of the Town until many years after the building of the Meeting House.

It was on the 6th* of December, 1717, that the Rev. Joseph Lamb was ordained as the

---

*The Salmon Record says the 4th, which is an error.

Minister of Mattituck by the Presbytery of
Long Island, which met, organized, and began
its existence at Southampton on the 17th of
April, 1717. The Mattituck Church was organized in 1715, two years before the ordination of its Pastor; and two years after his
ordination it asked to be taken under the
care of the Presbytery, and its request was
granted. Its first Pastor received ordination
the same year that he was graduated at Yale
College. His class numbered five graduates;
all became ministers—another indication which
shows how thoroughly Yale in its early years
was a Theological Seminary. The year of his
graduation was the year of the removal of the
College from Saybrook to New Haven. Like
the Rev. Benjamin Woolsey, who was graduated eight years earlier, Mr. Lamb occupied
the centre of the class in respect to social
standing.

He remained at Mattituck many years, and
his wife died there in April, 1729. He removed to Baskingridge, Somerset County,
New Jersey, previous to 1744, and on the
24th of May in this year he became a member of the Presbytery of New Brunswick.
Soon after his settlement in New Jersey, he

received into his congregation the Hon. Henry
Southard, who followed him from Long Island
to Baskingridge, which became the birthplace
of the Hon. Samuel L. Southard, one of the
most eminent and accomplished of the statesmen of New Jersey, who in the Cabinet of the
Nation successively performed the duties of
the Secretary of the Navy, of the Treasury,
and of War—who was successively Attorney
General and Governor of his native State;
and was repeatedly elected United States
Senator, and President of the Senate.

When Mr. Lamb became the Pastor of
Baskingridge, the worshippers met from Sabbath to Sabbath in a log-house, the first
church edifice ever erected in the place. But
the people under his ministry put up in 1749
a frame building far more commodious than
the old one; and this new structure continued in use for ninety years until 1839, when
it gave place to a stately brick edifice with a
tall and graceful spire. Mr. Lamb, however,
did not live to minister for many months in
the frame building. He died within the year
of its dedication, 1749.

The formation of the Mattituck Church and
the settlement of its Pastor and the prospect-

ive formation of a Church at Orient made an essential change in the ecclesiastical condition of the people of the Town. The citizens were not unmindful of this change.

Accordingly, in the Town Meeting of 1720, it was voted that three men be chosen to divide the parish lands proportionable, that each Minister may improve the same in proportion, according to the first purchase. Captain Reeve, Captain Booth and Benjamin Youngs were chosen. See Town Records, Book D, page 119. The Town Records do not indicate the method and effect of the division. But we may well suppose that there was assigned to the Mattituck Minister such a part of the parish lands as the property of his parishioners bore to the whole property of all the people who made the purchase and the early improvement of the Town. This was to be determined in some way by the conditions of the first purchase of the soil of the Town by its founders.

There seems to be in the Town Records no statement which marks the precise time when the Town ceased to collect and pay the minister's salary, or when the Town Meeting ceased to discipline church offenders. There

was doubtless a gradual preparation for the
change whereby the church ceased to be a
Town Church and became an Independent
Church. It did not become a Congregational
Church, in the present meaning of this term,
until a later period of its history.

No means of warming the church building
in cold weather had yet been provided and
used. Before the commencement of the public worship in the forenoon, as well as between
the forenoon and the afternoon services, and
sometimes also before the return home
towards the close of the Sabbath, the people
resorted to the private residences near the
church edifice, or to " The Public," in order
to warm themselves in front of the large and
open fire-places which a generous hospitality
kept well filled with blazing wood whenever
the temperature out of doors was low. But
the inconvenience of this bountiful hospitality
could not fail to be felt as a burden. Some
better method was requisite to enable those
who needed the use of food and of fire to
supply their wants at their own expense. It
was therefore voted by the Town Meeting to
allow Isaac Conkling to build a house for
convenience on the Lord's Day on the Town

lot.   This was one of the reforms accomplished in the early part of the Rev. Mr. Woolsey's
pastorate ; for this permission to build on the
Town lot a convenience-house was granted in
1722.   See Town Records, Book D, page
119.   These convenience-houses became in
later days comparatively numerous around
the church building.

During the Rev. Mr. Woolsey's ministry
the original church building ceased to be
needed and used for the purpose to which it
had been converted many years earlier ; and
hence it was, that in 1727 the Town Meeting
voted to sell the Prison House.

The edifice for public worship had now
ceased to be also a fortification, and subsequently a jail, and the expense of the public
worship was soon to be no more a tax assessed, collected and paid by the Town.

The County Court had been held once a
year in Southold and once a year in Southampton for some forty years from the formation of the county in 1683 ; but about 1727 a
court house, or county hall, was built at Riverhead, which was formerly in Southold, and
the court met in the new building for the first
time, March 27, 1729.

PART IV.

PERIOD AFTER THE MINISTRY OF THE REV. BENJAMIN WOOLSEY.

1736–1740.

CHAPTER VII.

In 1736, the Rev. Benjamin Woolsey removed from the Southold parsonage to the estate of his wife, in Oyster Bay township, Queens county, on the shore of Long Island Sound. It is a place of exceeding beauty. The gentle hills and slopes; the quiet valleys of no great extent; the fertile fields, rich with growing grain, or tinted with flowers of various hues, or enameled with luxuriant grasses; the magnificent trees, scattered here and there, or forming clumps of woods, or even considerable forests; and the bright, smooth lakes and bays, with the larger spaces of water visible on the Sound, all unite to present charming prospects in every direction. Mr. Woolsey called the place *Dos uxoris*, (the wife's dower), and by this name, contracted into Dosoris, it has ever since been known.

It is nearly two miles north of the village of Glen Cove, and immediately south of Matinecock Point on Long Island Sound. The original tract contained one thousand acres. It was bought of the Matinecock Indians by Robert Williams, who sold it to Lewis Morris, of the Island of Barbados, a brother of Richard Morris, the first owner of Morrisania, Westchester County, New York. Morris sold it, August 10, 1693, for £390, to Daniel Whitehead, of Oyster Bay, who conveyed it for the same price to his son-in-law, John Taylor, of Oyster Bay. Mr. Taylor bequeathed it to his only daughter, Abigail, whose husband named it in her honor, and she was well worthy of his supreme appreciation. He lived there at the head of a most generous and hospitable family for the last and best twenty years of his life, from 1736 to 1756. At his death, he devised three-fifths of it to his son, Colonel Melancthon Taylor Woolsey, and two-fifths to his son, Benjamin Woolsey, Jr. Nathaniel Coles bought the whole estate in 1760, paying £4,000 for the larger share and £3,600 for the smaller.

Mr. Woolsey was in his thirty-third year when he settled in Southold, and in his forty-

ninth when he removed to Dosoris. For the
next twenty years he ministered the gospel
at his own expense in various parishes. He
often preached in his own house, giving a
dinner also to the worshippers who came
from distant places. During a part of these
twenty years he supplied Hempstead on the
Sabbath. His gratuitous services were abundant not only in preaching on the Lord's Day,
but also in ministering to the sick and in conducting the solemnities at the burial of the
dead.

His devotion to his sacred duties is illustrated by the incident which the Rev. Dr.
Prime relates in the History of Long Island,
page 282, to attest the punctuality of this
good man to his engagements, and his un-
willingness to disappoint the expectations of
the congregation. During his ministry at
Hempstead, he was bereaved of a son, whose
death took place on a Saturday. Being unable to procure any person to supply his place
in the Hempstead pulpit, he deemed it to be
his heavy duty to leave his afflicted family on
the Sabbath, in order to fulfil his engagements. He did so, and performed his usual
services for the Hempstead congregation.

The Rev. Benjamin Woolsey died on the 15th of August, 1756. A few days later there appeared in "The Mercury" of New York, edited by Hugh Gaine, a tribute to his worth in which it was said, that "his intellectual powers were much above the common level, and were improved by a liberal education. His universal acquaintance with sacred literature rendered his public performances peculiarly edifying and instructive. His sentiments were just, noble and proper; his reasoning was clear and conclusive, and his pulpit eloquence manly, nervous and strong. The zeal and pathos that animated his discourses added peculiar grace and dignity to his address, and, while it engaged the attention of his hearers, discovered the sincere piety and fervent devotion that warmed and governed his own heart. He loved good men of every profession, and owned and admired sincere piety, under whatever form or denomination it appeared. Justice, charity and condescension, hospitality and public spirit, were virtues to which he paid the most sacred regard. In the discharge of the various duties which constitute the tender and affectionate husband, kind parent, the mild and gentle master, the obliging neighbor, the sincere, faithful and unshaken friend, he had few equals and no superiors."

He was buried at Dosoris, in the family cemetery, where fifteen years earlier he had buried his venerable father.

It was a fair, bright, lovely morning on the twenty-second day of May, 1872, when I visited Dosoris for the purpose of seeing the home of his later years and the place of his burial. During the previous night I had enjoyed by invitation the hospitality of the Rev. Benjamin L. Swan and his charming family, in the parsonage of the Presbyterian Church of Oyster Bay. He now gave me a seat in his carriage and became my guide to the spot which I desired to see. The drive from Oyster Bay to Dosoris, amid the exuberant life of the spring-time, with the air full of the fragrance of early flowers and vocal with the songs of rejoicing birds, is exceedingly delightful, especially in the company of a gentleman overflowing with courtesy, kindness, congeniality of taste and spirit, and great intelligence. So was my generous host. This made the day memorable. There is on the way an unceasing succession of various and attractive scenes of natural beauty—hills,

25

vales, fields, forests and streams, lakes and
bays, with here and there the wider prospects
of water on Long Island Sound, bearing upon
its peaceful bosom the shining sails of pleas-
ure and of commerce; and on the right hand
and the left many tasteful residences and cultivated grounds, crowning the hills, basking
on the slopes, and nestling in the valleys,
give animation and human interest to the
views.   The heavens also, during all that day,
were in harmony with the earth.   The greater part of the sky was a perfect blue; but
some spaces were flecked with clouds of ethe-
real forms and soft and gentle tones and hues.
The light breeze gave them wings, and their
graceful movements imparted, on this glorious day of spring-time, the charm of life and
activity to the ever-changing aspects of both
earth and heaven.   So many forms of beauty
can at once be rarely seen.

Dosoris was then owned and occupied by
Mr. George James Price. This gentleman
was that day absent from his home; but every
kind attention was shown by his family, and
especially by his father-in-law, Mr. Martin E.
Thompson, a very intelligent and active octo-
genarian, the architect of the former Mer-.

chants' Exchange of New York City and other handsome buildings which adorned the metropolis of the new world in the earlier stages of its wonderful life and growth in business, wealth, population and greatness. Mr. Thompson holds, with the utmost confidence, that notwithstanding the great changes made in the dwelling in 1842, the west end of the present large double two story-house, with a wide hall from south to north through the centre, must be, from the style, character and age of the architecture, and of the various carved-wood adornments, the very dwelling, in part at least, which was the home of the Rev. Benjamin Woolsey during the last twenty years of this good Minister's life. It was easy and grateful to yield one's mind and heart to the benign influence of the hallowed associations of the place.

The cemetery made sacred by the graves of many members of the family is in a grove of locusts trees on a knoll northeast of the residence. The land *makes* on the knoll, and the lower lines of many of the inscriptions are now some inches below the surface of the soil. Under the intelligent direction of Mr.

Thompson,* we read not a few of these inscriptions with living interest.   The following
is the inscription at the head of the most attractive grave :

SACRED TO THE MEMORY
OF THE REV'D. MR. BENJAMIN WOOLSEY
WHO
in the Vnited Character of the Gentleman, the Christian, the Divine
Shone with distinguish'd Lustre
and adorn'd every Station of public and private Life
with Dignity and Vsefulness.
Early devoted to the work of the Gospel Ministry,
Endow'd with the Gifts of Nature and Grace,
He employ'd his Superior Talents
In the service of his Divine Master
With Fidelity and Zeal.
After a shineing Course of Disinterested Labours
To promote the Cause of True Religion
He exchang'd the Ministry of the Church Militant on Earth
For the Reward of the Church Triumphant in Heaven
August 15th AD 1756 .E 69.

An excellent and remarkably complete ge-
nealogy of the descendants of the Rev. Ben-
jamin Woolsey, by Benjamin W. Dwight, Ph.
D., one of his posterity, was published in the
New York Genealogical and Biographical
Record.   See the fourth and fifth volumes,
July 1873—July 1874.   This publication is

*This accomplished and venerable gentleman died at
Dosoris, July 24, 1877, in the ninety-first year of his
age.   See New York Weekly Evening Post, August 1,
1877.

the authority for many of the statements in the following notices of some of his descendants. Only here and there in this country has lived a man whose descendants have been connected by blood and marriage with so many persons of great worth and distinction.

He had two sons and four daughters who grew up and married. His eldest son, Melancthon Taylor Woolsey, born June 8, 1717, married Rebekah Lloyd, and his eldest daughter, second of these children, Sarah Woolsey, born a year or two before his settlement in Southold, married John Lloyd. These Lloyds were children of Henry and Rebekah (Nelson) Lloyd, and their father had the ownership and occupancy of Lloyd's Neck, about three thousand acres between Cold Spring Harbor and Huntington Harbor, patented by Governor Dongan in 1685 with the rights and privileges of a manor named Queen's Village. Henry Lloyd was a son of James Lloyd, of Boston, and his wife Greselda Sylvester, of Shelter Island, whose lover, Latimer Sampson, gave her by his will one half of this tract of three thousand acres. After her marriage to James Lloyd, her husband bought the other half. After his death, his son Henry became the owner of the whole of

the peninsula and made it his home, in 1711.
It remains in the ownership and possession
of his descendants. The following letter of
Henry Lloyd, it has been said, discloses the
character both of persons and of times.

"Lloyd's Manor, Oct. 10, 1741.

"Sir :—As my son John has sometime made
suit to your daughter, Miss Sarah, I conclude
it is with your and Mrs. Woolsey's approbation ;
and, at his request, I hereby signify mine—
hoping if they come together, it may be to
their mutual happiness and with the good
liking of all concerned. His circumstances
being such as to enable him to live comforta-
bly without any immediate dependence on
me, I think little need be said on that head,
only thus far—as he is my son and has much
of my affection, I have, in the disposition of
what estate I possess, considered him as such,
without being over-concerned to make an elder son to the disinheriting of the younger
children. And I shall trust that Mrs. Woolsey and you will provide for Miss Sarah, as
your daughter.

I pray our best regards may be acceptable
to yourself and lady—not forgetting your
young lady.

I am, sir, your very humble servant,

H. LLOYD.

To the Rev. Benjamin Woolsey,
Dosoris, Long Island."

Melanĉthon Taylor Woolsey entered the army during the war against the French and Indians, had the rank of Colonel in the campaign of 1758, and died in the military service of his country at Crown Point, New York, September 28, 1758, in his forty-second year. He and his daughters Abigail, Elizabeth and Mary were buried at Dosoris. His daughter Rebekah, born August 22, 1755, married, October 10, 1782, James Hillhouse of New Haven, whose father was Judge William Hillhouse and whose mother, Sarah, was a sister of the first Governor Griswold of Connecticut. His grandfather was the Rev. James Hillhouse, whose wife was a granddaughter of the Rev. James Fitch, of Saybrook, and Priscilla, daughter of Capt. John Mason, the hero of the Pequot war.

Rebekah Woolsey's husband was graduated at Yale in 1773, a member of the State Legislature, Treasurer of Yale College fifty years, from 1782 to 1832, member of the U. S. House of Representatives six years, from 1790 to 1796, and thereafter U. S. Senator fourteen years, until 1810. He planted the elms which have given to New Haven the name of "The Elm City." His first wife was

Sarah Lloyd, daughter of John Lloyd and
Sarah Woolsey. She was born in 1753. The
husband of these two descendants of our third
pastor—being cousins—died December 29,
1832, aged 78 years. Probably no other man
has ever done as much for the beauty and
prosperity of New Haven as he did. His
wife Rebekah died December 30, 1813.

Among the Hillhouse descendants of our
third pastor were James A. Hillhouse, author
of "Percy's Masque," "Hadad," and other volumes ; and Rebekah Woolsey Hillhouse, first
wife of the Rev. Nathaniel Hewit, D. D., and
mother of the Rev. Nathaniel Augustus Hewit, D. D., an eloquent and celebrated preacher of the order of Paulists in the Roman Catholic Church.

Melancthon Lloyd Woolsey, son of Col.
Melancthon Taylor Woolsey and Rebekah
Lloyd, was born at Queen's Village, now
Lloyd's Neck, May 8, 1758. He became an
officer of the Revolutionary army as an aid to
Governor George Clinton. During the war,
on March 23, 1779, he married Alida, daugh-
ter of Henry Livingston, of Poughkeepsie,
whose wife Susan was a daughter of John
Conklin. Alida Livingston was a sister of the

Rev. John H. Livingston, D. D., who was the first Professor of Divinity of the Reformed Dutch Church and opened their first regular Theological Seminary in the United States, in 1795. This Institution of sacred learning began its beneficent work at Bedford, Long Island. In 1807 his Professorship was united to Rutgers College at New Brunswick, New Jersey, and he was continued in his office of Professor of Theology and also chosen to be the President of the College. His sister Alida, the wife of Gen. Woolsey, was the granddaughter of Gilbert Livingston, a grandson of the Rev. John Livingston, an energetic Minister of the gospel, who for the purity and excellence of his preaching was driven by the persecutions of the prelatical party from Scotland to Holland in 1663, and whose son Robert came to New York about 1675 and in 1686 received from Gov. Dongan the title to a large tract of land, including a great part of the present counties of Dutchess and Columbia, still known as Livingston Manor; for in 1715 George I. erected the manor and lordship of Livingston with the privilege of holding a court leet and a court baron, and with the right of advowson to all

the churches within its boundaries. Gen.
Woolsey retired from the army in 1780, but
afterwards became a Major General of the
State militia. He made his home at Cumber-
land Head, near Plattsburgh, was for many
years the Collector of the customs for the
Plattsburgh District, and also the Clerk of
Clinton county. He died at Trenton, New
York, June 29, 1819. His widow died at Os-
wego, July 12, 1843, aged 85 years.

Melancthon Taylor Woolsey, the first-born
of their eight children, six of whom grew up
and married, was born June 5, 1780. He entered the Navy of the United States in 1800,
fought under Com. Decatur against Tripoli,
and against England under Com. Chauncey in
the war of 1812. He commanded the U. S.
force at Oswego when the British were gal-
lantly repulsed at that point. He was afterwards transferred to the larger field of the
ocean service and commanded at the West
India Station, Pensacola, Fla., and subsequently commanded the Brazilian Squadron. He
married, Nov. 3, 1817, Susan Cornelia Treadwell, daughter of James Treadwell, of New
York. He died at his home in Utica, New
York, May 19, 1838. She died at Stamford,

Connecticut, March 13, 1863, in her sixty-seventh year. They had seven children, including Capt. Melancthon Brooks Woolsey, of the U. S. Navy, and Quartermaster Richard Lansing Woolsey, of the U. S. Army, as well as Alida Livingston Woolsey, wife of the Rev. Isaac Pierson Stryker, of New York City, and Mary Elizabeth Woolsey, wife of the Rev. Frank Windsor Braithwaite, of Stamford, Connecticut.

Our third pastor's second son, Benjamin, was born Feb. 12, 1720, the year of his settlement in Southold. This son was graduated at Yale in 1744, second in his class of fifteen, and next above the celebrated William Samuel Johnson, Judge of the Supreme Court of Connecticut, U. S. Senator, and President of Columbia College, New York City. Benjamin Woolsey, Jr., succeeded his father in the possession and occupancy of Dosoris, and was a magistrate of the colony for many years previous to his death, September 9, 1771. He married first Esther Isaacs, daughter of Ralph Isaacs, a merchant of Norwalk, Conn., and Mary Rumsey, daughter of Benjamin Rumsey, of Fairfield, Conn. Esther Isaacs Woolsey died March 29, 1756, aged twenty-

five years, about seven years after her marriage. Mr. Woolsey married a second wife,
Ann Muirson, daughter of Dr. George Muirson of Setauket and Anna Smith, daughter
of Judge Henry Smith, eldest son of William
Smith, Governor of Tangiers, Chief Justice of
New York, President of the Council and acting Governor of the Colony. Benjamin
Woolsey, Jr., had three children by his first
wife, namely, Sarah, who married Moses Rogers, one of three brothers, each of whom
founded a great mercantile house that continued forty years in New York, and two of
whose sisters were wives of eminent and
wealthy merchants in that city. Moses Rogers was Governor of the New York Hospital,
Director of the U. S. Bank, Treasurer of the
City Dispensary, Vestryman of Trinity Church,
and active in the Benevolent Societies of the
city. Their daughter Sarah Elizabeth Rogers
married the Hon. Samuel Miles Hopkins,
Member of the U. S. Congress, and founder
of the village of Moscow, New York, whose
children include William Rogers Hopkins,
Professor of Chemistry in the U. S. Naval
Academy at Annapolis, Maryland ; and the Rev.
S. M. Hopkins, D. D., who was graduated at

Amherst College in 1832, and at Auburn Theological Seminary in 1836, Pastor of the Presbyterian churches of Corning and of Fredonia, New York, and since 1847 Hyde Professor of Ecclesiastical History and Church Polity in Auburn Theological Seminary. One of his sons is the Rev. Abel Grosvenor Hopkins, who was graduated at Hamilton College in 1866 and at Auburn Theological Seminary in 1869, and is the Professor of the Latin Language and Literature in Hamilton College. Benjamin Woolsey Rogers, son of Moses and Sarah Woolsey Rogers, was a large importer of hardware in New York, thirty-eight years a Governor of the New York Hospital, and one of the founders of the Bloomingdale Asylum. His daughter Sarah married William P. Van Rensselaer, son of Stephen Van Rensselaer of Albany, the Patroon. His son Benjamin Woolsey married a daughter of Dr. Richard Kissam Hoffman, a celebrated surgeon of New York City, and their son Hoffman married a daughter of the Hon. John Ferdon, of Piermont, New York. Another son of Moses and Sarah Woolsey Rogers, Archibald Rogers, married a daughter of Judge Nathaniel Pendleton, an

26

intimate friend of Alexander Hamilton and
his second in the fatal duel with Aaron Burr.
Archibald Rogers's son Edmund Pendleton
Rogers is the proprietor of the "Quintard
Iron Works" in New York, and his daughter
Susan Bard Rogers is the wife of Herman,
son of John T. Livingston, who owns a line
of steamers hailing from New York.

Benjamin, son of Benjamin and Esther
Isaacs Woolsey, died in his fifth year.

Their daughter Mary married the Rev.
Timothy Dwight, D. D., President of Yale
College. She died October 5, 1845, aged
ninety-one years. President Dwight was a
son of Major Timothy Dwight and Mary,
daughter of the Rev. Jonathan Edwards, D.
D., President of the College of New Jersey.
He was born May 14, 1752, and died January
11, 1817. Among their very many descendants are the Rev. Edward Strong Dwight,
Pastor of Hadley, Massachusetts ; Benjamin
Woolsey Dwight, M. D., Treasurer of Hamilton College, and his celebrated sons, Benjamin Woodbridge Dwight, Ph. D., who was
graduated at Hamilton College in 1835, the
distinguished teacher, author and genealogist,
and Theodore William Dwight, LL. D., who

was graduated at Hamilton College in 1840, the learned and eloquent Professor in the Law Department of Columbia College, New York city; the Rev. Timothy Dwight, D. D., who was graduated at Yale in 1849, the Professor of Greek Exegesis in the Theological Department of Yale College and one of the Revisers of the New Testament; the Rev. Sereno Edwards Dwight, D. D., who was graduated at Yale in 1803, married in 1811, Susan Edwards, daughter of Judge David Daggett, of New Haven, and was President of Hamilton College; the Rev. William Theodore Dwight, D. D., who was graduated at Yale in 1813, and was for thirty-two years pastor of the Third Congregational Church of Portland, Maine; Henry Edwin Dwight, M. D., who was graduated at Yale in 1852, a prominent physician of Philadelphia, Pa.; Thomas Bradford Dwight, who was graduated at Yale in 1859, a lawyer of Philadelphia, Pa.

Our third pastor's son Benjamin had seven children by his second wife. Of these children, Esther, born at Dosoris, December 1, 1759, married Capt. Palmer of the British army and died at Raphoe, Ireland, March 15, 1807. William Walton Woolsey, son of Benjamin

Woolsey, Jr., and his second wife, Ann Muirson, was born September 17, 1766, and married April 2, 1792, Elizabeth Dwight, sister
of President Dwight of Yale College, whose
wife, Mary Woolsey, was a half sister of William Walton Woolsey. He was a prosperous
merchant of New Haven, Connecticut, and
had the charge of many trusts and filled many
public offices. He had seven children, and
his posterity include Mary Anne Woolsey,
who married Jared Scarborough, a graduate
of Yale and a merchant of Hartford, Connecticut, whose son William Woolsey Scarborough is a merchant of Cincinnati and President of the Bank of the Ohio Valley. Jared
Scarborough died in 1816 and his widow
married for a second husband the Hon.
George Hoadley, who was graduated at Yale,
a lawyer of New Haven, Mayor of the City
and President of the Eagle Bank. When he
was nearly fifty years of age he became in
1830 a resident of Cleveland, Ohio, and became the Mayor thereof. He died there in
1857, aged 75 years. Their daughter, Mary
Ann Hoadley, married Thomas Fuller Pomeroy, a graduate of Union College, and a physician of Detroit, Michigan. Another daugh-

ter, Elizabeth Dwight Hoadley, married the Hon. Joshua Hall Bates, a graduate of West Point, Lieutenant in the U. S. Army in the Florida war, and Brigadier General from April to August, 1861, in the war against the Rebellion. Their son George Hoadley was graduated at the Western Reserve College in 1844, a lawyer in Cincinnati, Ohio, twice Judge of the Supreme Court of Hamilton County, and since 1864 Professor of Commercial Law in the Cincinnati Law School.

Elizabeth Woolsey, daughter of W. W. Woolsey and Elizabeth Dwight, married Francis Bayard Winthrop, Jr., a graduate of Yale and a lawyer of New Haven, Ct. Their son, Major Theodore Winthrop, was graduated at Yale, an author, an officer in the late war, and killed at Big Bethel, Va., June 10, 1861. Their son, Major William Woolsey Winthrop, was graduated at Yale, a lawyer, and Assistant to Judge Advocate Holt in the late war. Their daughter, Sarah Chauncey Winthrop, married in 1861 Theodore Weston, a graduate of Yale, a civil engineer in New York, employed on the Croton Water Works.

John Mumford Woolsey, son of W. W. Woolsey and Elizabeth Dwight, was gradua-

ted at Yale in 1813, married a daughter of
Dr. John Andrews of Wallingford, Connecticut, and was a hardware merchant in New
York, and subsequently a capitalist in Cleveland, Ohio. He died at New Haven, Connecticut, July 11, 1870, aged seventy-four
years, and was buried at Dosoris, Long Isl-
and. His daughter Sarah Chauncey Woolsey
is the popular writer known as " Susan Cool-
idge." His other daughter, Jane Woolsey, is
the wife of the Rev. Henry Albert Yardley, a
graduate of Yale, tutor there, and subsequently Professor in the Episcopal Theological
Seminary at Middletown, Connecticut.

William Cecil Woolsey, twin with John
Mumford Woolsey, was graduated in the
same class with him at Yale in 1813, and married in 1829 Catharine Rebekah, daughter of
Gen. Theodorus Bailey of New York. He
was an auctioneer in New York. His daughter Ann Eliza married Samuel Fisher Carmalt, a large land owner at Lake Wyalusing,
Pa. His son William Walton Woolsey, M.
D., studied medicine at Yale and became a
physician at Dubuque, Iowa.

Laura Woolsey, daughter of Wm. W.
Woolsey, married Samuel William Johnson, a

graduate of Union College, a resident of
Stratford Conn. Her son Samuel William
Johnson was graduated at the College of New
Jersey in 1849 and at the Law Department of
Harvard College in 1851. Her daughter
Laura Woolsey Johnson married Dr. William
Henry Carmalt, a brother of the husband of
her cousin Ann Eliza Woolsey. Her son
Woolsey Johnson, M. D., was graduated at
the College of New Jersey in 1860 and at the
New York Medical College in 1863. He is
a physician in New York City.

Theodore Dwight Woolsey, D. D., LL.
D., son of W. W. Woolsey and Elizabeth
Dwight, was born October 31, 1801, graduated at Yale in 1820 and then tutor there
three years. After studying theology in
Princeton and New Haven, he gave several
years to study and travel in Europe until
1830. The next year he became the Professor of the Greek Language and Literature in
Yale College and continued in this Professorship twenty years. For twenty-five years he
was President of Yale, and then resigned the
Presidency, but continues to give instruction
in three of the departments of the college.
He is a voluminous author, President of the

Evangelical Alliance, and President of the
New Testament Revisers of the Bible. His
daughter Agnes is the wife of the Rev. Ed-
gar Laing Heermance, Pastor of the Presbyterian Church of White Plains, New York,
who is a son of the Rev. Henry Heermance
of Kinderhook, New York. President Woolsey's son, Theodore Salisbury Woolsey, LL.
B., is Professor of International Law in Yale
College.

President Woolsey's sister Sarah married
Charles Frederick Johnson, a lawyer by profession, an amateur farmer by occupation,
at Owego, New York. Their eldest son,
Charles Frederick, was graduated at Yale in
1855, was assistant Professor of Mathematics
in the U. S. Naval Academy from 1865 to
1870, and is the Superintendent of the Bristol
Iron Works, Owego, New York. He married a daughter of the Hon. William J. Mc
Alpine, of Pittsfield, Massachusetts.

The second son of Charles Frederick and
Sarah Woolsey Johnson is William Woolsey
Johnson, who was graduated at Yale in 1862,
Assistant Professor of Mathematics in the U.
S. Naval Academy from 1864 to 1869, then
Professor of Mathematics in Kenyon College,

Gambier, Ohio, and since 1872 Professor of Mathematics in St. John's College, Annapolis, Maryland.

Elizabeth Woolsey, daughter of Benjamin Woolsey, Jr., and Ann Muirson married William Dunlap, who bore the colors of the 47th Regiment, " Wolfe's Own," on the Plains of Abraham, when Wolfe gained the great victory and died. William Dunlap was a voluminous author, and among his books are a Biography of Charles Brockden Brown, The Arts of Design in the United States, and The History of the New Netherlands. He was a pupil of Benjamin West, and is best known as a painter.

Our third pastor's grandson, George Muirson Woolsey, son of Benjamin, married Abby, daughter of Joseph Howland. He was largely engaged in shipping in New York, owned Green Hook, Long Island, and died at his country-seat in Newtown, Long Island. His son Charles William Woolsey perished in the Lexington on Long Island Sound, January 13, 1840, leaving a widow and eight children, the eldest twelve years old. His daughter Mary Elizabeth Watts is the wife of the Rev. Dr. Robert S. Howland, Rector of the Church of the Heavenly Rest, Fifth Avenue, New

York. His daughter Georgiana Muirson is
the wife of Francis Bacon, who was graduated
M. D. at Yale, and is the Professor of Sur-
gery in that College—a son of the Rev. Leonard Bacon, D. D., L.L. D. Charles Wm. Woolsey's daughter Eliza Newton married Col·
Joseph Howland, an author and amateur
farmer at Matteawan, New York. Another
daughter of the same family, Harriet Roose-
velt, married Dr. Hugh Lenox Dodge, L.L.
D., Professor in the Medical Department of
the University of Pennsylvania—the brother
of the Rev. Charles Dodge D. D., LL. D.
Another daughter, Caroline Carson, married
Edward Mitchell, a graduate of Columbia
College, a lawyer of New York, son of Judge
William Mitchell of that city. The son of
Charles William Woolsey, Col. Charles Wil-
liam Woolsey, married Arixene Southgate
Smith, eldest daughter of Henry B. Smith,
D. D., LL. D., Professor of Theology in the
Union Theological Seminary, New York City,
one of the foremost of American scholars,
thinkers, authors, and his wife Elizabeth Lee,
his biographer, daughter of William Allen, D.
D., President of Bowdoin College.   Col.

Woolsey is a gentleman farmer at Briar Cliff, near Sing Sing, New York.

Our third pastor's grandson George Muirson Woolsey had a son, Edward John Woolsey, who married Emily Phillips Aspinwall, sister of William H. Aspinwall and John Lloyd Aspinwall, New York, and who died at Astoria, Long Island, June 30, 1873, aged 71 years, leaving to his son Edward John Woolsey, Jr., one hundred thousand dollars and his real estate in Newtown, Long Island, with the furniture, books, pictures, wines, crops and farm utensils and stock, and a farm and island adjoining, with other property; and to his wife all the rest of his real and personal estate, including a country seat at Lenox, Massachusetts, one of the finest in the State.

Our third Pastor's second daughter, Hannah, married Samuel McCoun of Oyster Bay, Long Island.

The third daughter, Mary, married, first, Platt Smith, and, after his death, Dr. George Muirson of Setauket, Long Island.

The fourth daughter, Abigail, married the Rev. Dr. Noah Welles, a celebrated divine and author, the rector of the church of Stamford, Connecticut.

But two of Pastor Woolsey's children who married were sons. Most of his descendants are in the feminine branches of the family, and these are perhaps not less eminent and fruitful than the male branches.

Among the distinguished names in these branches are those of Lt. Gov. John Broome ; Dr. James Cogswell; Chancellor William T. McCoun ; Hon. Samuel McCoun ; Rear-Admiral Samuel Livingston Breese, U. S. Navy; Hon. Sidney Breese, Chief Justice of the Supreme Court of Illinois, U. S. Senator ; Sarah Elizabeth Griswold, wife of Samuel Finley Breese Morse, LL. D., inventor of the telegraph ; Susan Breese, wife of the Rev. Dr. Pierre Alexis Proal ; Arthur Breese, U. S. Navy ; Hon. Peter W. Radcliff ; Mary Welles Davenport, wife of James Boorman of New York ; Rev. John Sidney Davenport; Julia Davenport Wheeler, wife of Selah Brewster Strong, Esq., of St. George's Manor, Setauket, L. I.; Rev. James Radcliff Davenport; Dr. Benjamin Welles; Rev. Benjamin Welles ; George Welles McClure, U. S. Army ; Henry Welles, twenty-one years Judge of the Supreme Court of New York ; Sarah Haight Welles, wife of the Hon. Thomas A. Johnson, Judge

of the Supreme Court of New York; Mary
Eliza and Helen Lydia Welles, successively
wives of William Johnson, President of the
New Haven City Bank and of the New Ha-
ven and Northampton Railroad; Abigail
Woolsey Welles, wife of the Rev. Dr. Henry
Gilbert Ludlow, and mother of the well known
authors, Fitzhugh and Helen Welles Ludlow.

After the removal of the Rev. Benjamin
Woolsey to Dosoris, the church of Southold
was destitute of a pastor for two years; but
on the 26th of October, 1738, an ecclesiastical council ordained and installed the Rev.
James Davenport as its Pastor.

His great-grandfather had been a celebrated minister in London, England, and also in
Holland, was the chief founder of the City
and the Colony of New Haven, where he was
the first Minister of the Church. After the
New Haven Colony became identified with
that of Connecticut, under the charter of the
latter, a union which he had most strenuously
resisted on behalf of the New Haven Colony,
and which was very unsatisfactory to himself,
he accepted a call to be the Pastor of the
First Church of Boston, Massachusetts, in
which office he died. He was one of the

greatest, best and most influential men in the early history of New England.

The father of our fourth Pastor was the Rev. John Davenport, who was graduated at Harvard College in 1687 and ordained and installed the Pastor of Stamford, Connecticut, in 1694, and died in this office on the fifth of February, 1731, aged sixty-one years, having been an eminently faithful and useful minister, and so familiar with the original languages of the Bible that he was accustomed to use them, and not a translation into English, in his family worship.

His son James was born in Stamford, when his father had become forty years of age, in 1710, was graduated at Yale College in 1732, second in social position in a class of twenty-three, of whom nine became Ministers of the Gospel. During three years of his College course, two Southold men pursued their studies with him in Yale, namely, Simon Horton and Abner Reeve, who were graduated one year preceding him. Though he was twenty-two years of age at the time of his graduation, he continued to reside in New Haven for several years thereafter, and during this period he pursued his preparation for the gospel ministry with so much ardor and devotion that his health was greatly impaired. He put himself under the medical treatment of Dr. Hubbard of that city, but this physician's skill seeming to be inadequate to the case, he went to Killingworth, Connecticut, and became a member of the family of the Rev. Dr. Jared Eliot—justly celebrated both as a physician and a minister—in order that he might have the benefit of his medical knowledge and prescriptions. In this way, after a few months, he so far recovered his health that he was able to return to New Haven and resume his studies. But this early breaking down of his health prepared the way for subsequent ailments and diseases which greatly affected both his body and his mind, and caused most unhappy and painful consequences to himself and to others during the later years of his pastoral relation to the Church of Southold, from which he was not released until 1744. Throughout the two earlier years of his ministry here, there was little departure from the orderly and faithful attention to his pastoral duties and little want of the satisfactory performance thereof; for in these earlier years there was no serious failure of his health—no prostration of his reason and judgment by overpowering mental and physical maladies. When the first century of the History of Southold closed, in 1740, he had not become deeply involved in those erratic and irrational proceedings for which he has been severely re- proached, and somewhat unjustly blamed, be- cause sufficient allowance has not been gen- erally made for the effects of the diseases from which he was suffering in mind and body, and which rendered him in the just judgment of the Civil Court of Boston *non compos mentis*, and therefore not guilty, even though it was evident that he had, in the denunciation of good men, committed offences which a per- son of sound mind could not have committed without making himself worthy of condemna- tion and liable to punishment.

In the spring of 1738 his ministry was de- sired at Maidenhead and Hopewell, now Law- renceville and Pennington, New Jersey, and the Presbytery of Philadelphia wrote to him in behalf of those congregations ; but, as the Rev. Dr. Sprague says in his " Annals of the American Pulpit," Vol. 3, p. 81, " he received a call from Southold, Long Island, about the same time, to which he gave the preference.

Southold was the oldest town on the Island, and had been left vacant, in 1736, by the removal of the Rev. Benjamin Woolsey. His ordination took place on the 26th of October, 1738. Among the ministers composing the council was his brother-in-law, the Rev. (afterwards Dr.) Stephen Williams of Longmeadow."

The Rev. Richard Webster, in his " History of the Presbyterian Church in America," makes essentially the same statements respecting Mr. Davenport, thus : " He seems to have preached in New Jersey in the close of 1737; for Philadelphia Presbytery gave leave, March 12, 1738, to Maidenhead and Hopewell, (Lawrence and Pennington,) to send for him, and also wrote a letter for them to him. He preferred to settle at Southold, the oldest town on Long Island, left vacant in 1736 by the removal of Mr. Woolsey, and was ordained by a council, Oct. 26th, 1738."

The remarkable career of this famous man in the later years of his pastoral relation to the First Church of Southold, is worthy of full and careful narration ; but the narrative does not properly belong to the history of the First Century of this place, and must wait for

another volume.   It will for the present suf-
fice to add, that his wayward and turbulent
course continued as long as he was under the
control of those maladies, which made him, in
the judgment of good sense and charitable
construction, not responsible for his enthusi-
asm, bitterness, fanatical errors and unjust
denunciations of good men, in all of which he
followed in the footsteps of Whitefield, but
not with equal rashness and culpability.

The latest years of his life were marked by
humility of heart, sweetness of disposition,
and a becoming sobriety of temper and judgment.   And it should not be overlooked, that
these latest years were devoted to the spiritual welfare of " the people of Maidenhead and
Hopewell " in the very place where his services were desired twenty years before the date
of his death and just before his settlement in
Southold.   He died while he was the pastor
of the New Side Presbyterian church of Hopewell, whose house of worship stood about a
mile west of Pennington.   He was buried in
the cemetery which marks the site where this
church edifice, now gone, formerly stood.

On the eighteenth of May, 1877, I visited
this hallowed ground.   By the kindness of

the Rev George Hale, D. D., former Pastor
of the First Presbyterian Church of Pennington and now Secretary of the General Assembly's Board of Ministerial Relief, I became
the guest of the Rev. Daniel R. Foster, the
present Pastor of that church, whose abundant hospitality included a drive in his comfortable carriage to this old cemetery of the
" New Side" Presbyterians of the neighborhood in Colonial times. The day was warm
for the month of May, the temperature being
90° in the shade. The cemetery fronts towards
the south or southwest. There is a bluff a
few feet high between it and the carriage
way in the public road that passes by it. On
the same general level with the top of this
low bluff is the greater part of the burying
ground, which slopes down very gently
towards the east. In front of the cemetery
is a substantial wall as high as a man's waist,
and distant perhaps two rods from the edge
of the bluff at the side of the road. This
space of ground between the edge of the
bluff and the wall, and extending the whole
length of the cemetery, is beautifully covered
with natural sward, in which grow a few large
and noble trees—a maple, two or three white

oaks and as many black walnuts. The effects
of age and of storms can be seen upon the
maple. There are also a few fine trees within the sacred grounds. North or north-west
of Mr. Davenport's grave—a rod distant from
its side—is a magnificent elm. Another
somewhat more remote from the foot of the
tomb lifts its noble form high into the air.
The marble over the grave is a large horizontal slab, and the inscription is carefully and
neatly cut. The marble rests on a substruct-
ure of brick-work, in which a few of the bricks
at the head of the grave have become dis-
placed.

On the south of the grave is that of Mrs.
Davenport, marked with a vertical stone at
the head, which is towards the west, and the
inscription is on the west face of the stone.
The lettering is neat and legible.

The land on every side for a mile away is
fertile and well cultivated. Many single trees
stand here and there in fields, or along the
lines of fences ; enough to give to the scene
in a warm day the aspect of retirement, fresh-
ness and repose. The effect is heightened
by the circumstance, that but few dwellings or

other buildings stand nearer than half a mile from the cemetery.

The inscriptions are as follows:

IN MEMORY OF

The Revd. JAMES DAVENPORT

WHO DEPARTED THIS LIFE

NOVR. 10TH 1757,

AGED 40 YEARS.

Oh Davenport, a Seraph once in Clay,
A brighter Seraph now in heavenly Day,
How glow'd thy Heart, with sacred Love and zeal !
How like to that thy kindred Angels feel !
Cloth'd in Humility, thy Virtues shone,
In every eye illustrious but thine own.
How like thy Master, on whose friendly Breast
Thou oft hast lean'd, and shalt forever rest !

IN

IN MEMORY OF

PARNEL WIFE OF

THE REVD

JAMES DAVENPORT

WHO DEPARTED THIS LIFE

AUGUST 21ST 1789

AGED 60 YEARS.

Mr. Davenport had one son, John, who was born at Philippi, New Jersey, August 11, 1752, graduated at the College of New Jersey in 1769, being a classmate with the Rev. Dr. Matthias Burnett, Gov. John Henry of Maryland, and the Rev. Dr. Samuel Stanhope

Smith, President of the College. He studied for the ministry under the Rev. Dr. Joseph Bellamy, of Bethlehem, Connecticut, and also under the Rev. Dr. Samuel Buell, of Easthampton, Long Island. In his early life he was an intimate friend of Aaron Burr, and while pursuing his theological studies under Dr. Buell, he wrote to Burr, who was residing with Dr. Bellamy, and made known his desire, that this ambitious man would give himself to the ministry of the gospel. He said: " I hope you are by this time fully resolved to engage in the sacred work of the ministry, and that you see your way clear to do it. You are placed under a very judicious as well as pious divine, whose instruction and conversation have, I hope, proved to your spiritual benefit. I rejoice to find you are pleased with your situation, and wish it may continue." John Davenport was ordained at Easthampton, Long Island, by the Presbytery of Suffolk County, on the fifteenth of June, 1774. The Rev. Messrs. John Storrs, Ebenezer Prime, Samuel Buell, James Brown, Joshua Hart and David Rose took part in the service. He remained in the Presbytery of Suffolk County until April 12, 1786, when he was dismissed to accept a call to be the Pastor of the church at Bedford, Westchester County, New York. While he remained on the Island he ministered chiefly at Mattituck. After his ministry at Bedford, he was installed as the Pastor of the church in Deerfield, Cumberland County, New Jersey, August 12, 1795, and was released on account of ill health in October, 1805. He returned to the State of New York in 1809, and died at Lysander, Onondaga County, July 13, 1821, in the 69th year of his age. He had a sister older than himself. Her name was Elizabeth. She married Mr. Enos Kelsey, a merchant of Princeton, New Jersey, where they lived and died. Their graves are in the Princeton cemetery.

Throughout the later periods of the First Century of Southold the civil government was orderly and peaceful. The royal province, after the departure of Cornbury, was under the administrations of Gov. John Lovelace, 1708–1710; Gov. Robert Hunter, 1710–1719; Gov. William Burnet, 1720–1727; Gov. John Montgomerie, 1728–1731; Gov. William Cosby, 1732–1736; Lieut. Gov. George Clarke, 1736–1743. The members of the Assembly from Suffolk were William Nicholl, 1701–

1723, Speaker, in 1702–1716; Samuel Mulford, 1705–1720; Samuel Hutchinson, 1721–1737; Epenetus Platt, 1723–1739.

Autograph of Samuel Hutchinson in 1721.

For the county administration in this period the County Judges were successively Joseph Fordham, who succeeded our Isaac Arnold, and Henry Smith. The Surrogates, Joseph Fordham, Jekamiah Scott, Brindley Sylvester and Henry Smith. The Sheriffs were Richard Floyd, 1708, John Brush, Daniel Sayre, Joshua Horton, Joseph Wickham, Daniel Youngs, Samuel Dayton, William Sell, Joseph Smith, David Corey, Jacob Conklin, and in 1740, Thomas Higbie. The County Clerks were Andrew Gibb, C. Congreve, Samuel Hudson and William Smith. In this period Shelter Island became detached from Southold in the civil administration of Town affairs. It had hitherto been a part of the Town of Southold in political organization as well as

in church relations. But in 1730 it was erected into a separate corporation, having at that
time twenty men who were of full age, namely :
Joel Bowditch, John Bowditch, Daniel Brown,
Thomas Conklin, Edward Gilman, Edward
Havens, George Havens, Henry Havens,
John Havens, Jonathan Havens, Joseph Havens, Samuel Hopkins, Samuel Hudson, Sylvester L'Hommedieu, William Nicholl, Abraham Parker, Elisha Paine, Brindley Sylvester,
Noah Tuthill and Samuel Vail. Some of
these persons, especially William Nicholl and
Brindley Sylvester, like wealthy men on all
parts of Long Island, owned many negro
slaves. Their first Town Meeting was held
April 7, 1730, and William Nicholl was chos-
en Supervisor; John Havens and Samuel
Hudson, Assessors ; Edward Havens, Collect-
or ; and Edward Gilman, Clerk.

In 1733 they built a church edifice with a
view to the uses of the Town and the formation of a Presbyterian Church. The congregation was incorporated under the law of the
State on the 26th of April, 1785, when John N.
Havens, Sylvester Deering and William Bowditch were elected Trustees ; but the church
was not fully organized until 1808. Brindley

28

Sylvester, son of Nathaniel Sylvester, was a grandson of that Nathaniel Sylvester, who in 1674 became the owner of the whole of Shelter Island. This Brindley Sylvester maintained his own private Chaplain, the Licentiate William Adams, a son of the Rev. Eliphalet Adams, of New London. But Mr. Sylvester's church membership was in the Southold church and here he worshipped habitually, and his family also, every Sabbath day. His boat was rowed for this purpose by four men or by six men according to the condition of wind, tide and weather. On the death of Mr. Sylvester, whose funeral was conducted by the Rev. William Throop, Pastor of Southold, and the sermon printed in Boston, the Licentiate William Adams became in 1752 the Chaplain of Thomas Deering, son-in-law of Mr. Sylvester. It was in 1737 that Mr. Sylvester erected his dwelling, which is now the summer residence of Prof. Eben N. Horsford, Mrs. Horsford, a daughter of the late Samuel S. Gardiner, Esq., being an heir through the Havens and the L'Hommedieu families. It was in part built of materials imported from England and used in the construction of his grandfather's residence in 1670. In 1695

Brindley Sylvester's uncle Giles Sylvester sold one fourth of the Island to William Nicholl for £500, and by will in 1720 he gave him another quarter of it. In 1695, also, Brindley Sylvester's father sold one thousand acres in the centre of the Island to George Havens, a Welshman.

This separation of Shelter Island from Southold in its political organization was the chief event in the civil affairs of the old Town in the later periods of its First Century.

From 1694 until the present day the principal civil officer of the Town has been the Supervisor. During the first half of the last century this office was filled successively by John Tuthill, Benjamin Youngs, Thomas Mapes, James Reeve, Samuel Hutchinson, Samuel Beebe, James Fanning, Thomas Reeve, Joshua Youngs, and Samuel Landon; by the latter from 1739 to 1752.

In these orderly and peaceful times, the people were virtuous, diligent and prosperous, increasing in number, intelligence and wealth. They well maintained the good character of the Church and Town.

INDEX.

Clark, Richard, an early settler, 45.
Clarke, Samuel, bill of, for building the Meeting House gallery, 233.
Clerks of the county, 324.
Cleveland, Benjamin, Genealogy of, 122.
Cleveland, Deacon Moses C., residence of, 198.
Code, Biblical, knowledge of, in Southold, 99.
Coe, Judge Benjamin, 264, 265.
Coke, Sir Edward, contemporary with the founders of Southold, 74.
Colbert, statesman of France, 195.
Colve, Capt. Anthony, Governor of New York, character and administration of, 141 ; his authority declined by the East End, 141, 142; letter of, to the Governor of Connecticut, 160.
Commerce in the early years of Southold, 77.
Commissioners of Emigration, 18, 19.
Commissioners of the Dutch visit the East End, 158; and return to New York, 159.
Common and undivided lands, laws relating to, 209-211.
Commoners' incorporation, 209, 210.
Conklin, David T., residence of, east of Capt. John Underhill's original home-lot, 85.
Conklin, Jacob and Samuel, bills of, for Meeting House banisters, 233.
Conklin, Jacob, an early settler, 45,
Conklin, John, an early settler, removed to Huntington, 33, 45.
Conklin, John, Jr., an early settler, 45 ; tomb-stone of, 122.
Connecticut, boundaries of, extended over the New Haven Colony, 68 ; charter of, 130; appointed its Governor and Capt. John Youngs of Southold to settle the English Plantations on Long Island, but soon disclaimed these towns, 131-133.
Convenience houses, 281, 282.
Cooper, John, an early settler of Southampton, 31 ; in Southold warns the Dutch, 157, 158.
Cooper, Thomas, an early settler of Southold, 45.
Corey, Abraham, an early settler, 45.
Corey, Jacob, born perhaps in Southold, 33 ; lived here before pastor Youngs's death, 45 ; an appraiser of the pastor's estate, 115 ; and died here in 1706.
Corey, John, an early settler, 45.

29

England, 28; after 1640 lived and died in Southold,
29; an early settler, 46; site of his home-lots, 84;
description of his tomb-stone, 122.
Horton, Benjamin, an early settler, 46.
Horton, Caleb, an early settler, 46.
Horton, David P., residence of, on the original home-
lots of Barnabas Horton, 84.
Horton, George F., M. D., author of the "Horton Gen-
ealogy," 29.
Horton, Jonathan, Jr., father of the Rev. Azariah Hor-
ton, 265.
Horton, Joseph, an early settler, 46.
Horton, Joshua, appraiser of the first Pastor's estate,
115.
Horton, Rev. Simon, born in the old Horton house, 263;
sketch of, 263-265.
Horton, Theodore K., visit of, to Mouseley, England, 122.
Horton, Deacon William, presided at the first election of
Trustees of the First Church, 231.
Hospitality in winter to Church-goers, 281.
Houldsworth, Jonas, an early settler who removed to
Huntington, 46.
Howe, Capt. Daniel, a planter of Southampton, 31.
Howe, John, contemporary with the founders of South-
old, 76.
Howell, George R., historian of Southampton, 31; un-
historic claim of, that Southampton is the oldest
Town on Long Island, 40.
Howell, Richard, an early settler, 46.
Hubbard, Rev. John, of Jamaica, generosity and suffer-
ing of, 238.
Hunter, Col. Robert, Governor of New York, arrests
persecution and gives Southold an opportunity to
build a new Meeting House, 239; controversy with
Episcopal Ministers, 258.
Huntington submits to the Dutch, 152.
Hutchinson, Samuel, member of Assembly, etc., auto-
graph of, 324.
Hutchinson, Thomas, an early settler, 46; delegate from
Southold to confer with the Dutch conquerors, 146;
declined to be a magistrate of Southold under the
Dutch government, 157.
Huntting, Edward, residence of, on the original home-
lot of Barnabas Wines, 85.

Sturgis, Richard S., residence of, on the original home
lot of Richard Benjamin, 198.
Style, change of, from old to new, 179.
Suffolk county formed in 1683 and court house built in
Riverhead some forty-four years later, 282.
Sunderland, Matthew, on the 18th of June, 1639, rented
land in Southold, and cultivated it, paying rent in
September, 1639, and in the next September, 36, 37.
Supervisors, 327.
Surinam exchanged for New York, 160.
Surrogates, 324.
Swan, Rev. Benjamin L., hospitality of, 289.
Sweeping the Meeting House, bill for, 233.
Swezey, John, an early settler, 47 ; ancestor of the Hon.
William H. Seward and others, 55.
Swezey, Rev. Samuel, pastor at Chester, N. J., 275, 276.
Sylvester, Joshua, an early settler, 47.
Sylvester, Capt. Nathaniel, of Shelter Island, hospital-
ity of, 154, 155.

Tax lists, 184-187, 217-220.
Taxes, how assessed and paid, 95.
Taylor, Jeremy, contemporary with the founders of
Southold, 76.
Taylor, John and wife, 257.
Terrell, Thomas, an early settler, 47.
Terry, Daniel, an early settler, 47.
Terry, Hiram J., residence of, on the original home lot
of Philemon Dickerson, 85.
Terry, John, an early settler, 47.
Terry, Jonathan B., wharf of, 91.
Terry, Richard, an early settler, 47 ; Recorder, 199.
Terry, Stuart T., residence of, 156.
Terry, Thomas, an early settler, 47 , site of his home lot
south of Barnabas Wines's, where Patrick May
now lives, 85 ; came in 1635 with his brothers
Robert and Richard from England, 30.
Thirty years' war, 73.
Thompson, Benjamin F., statement of, 26.
Thompson, Martin E., courtesy of, 290 ; death of, 292.
Throop, Rev. William, fifth pastor of Southold, sermons
of, 260, 326.
Tillotson, John, contemporary with the founders of
Southold, 76.
30

www.ingramcontent.com/pod-product-compliance
Lightning Source LLC
Chambersburg PA
CBHW021106270326
41929CB00009B/749